The Autonomous Enterprise

The Autonomous Enterprise

Governance, Decision Rights, and the Frameworks That Separate the Pacesetters from Everyone Else

Justus Daniel Eapen
Former Chief Information Officer

ORCHESTRIS AUTONOMOUS IT

The Integrated Risk and AI Governance Maturity Model and its diagnostic patterns (Documentation Theater, Locked-In, Unmodeled, Misaligned) are the author's proprietary frameworks. Appendix A presents selected representative questions to illustrate the framework's diagnostic logic. The complete assessment instrument, scoring methodology, triangulation discipline, and engagement process remain proprietary and are used only in formal advisory work. Appendix B presents a notional sample maturity profile illustrating the form of the engagement output; it does not derive from any specific client engagement.

Case studies and anecdotes have been constructed as composites drawn from patterns observed across executive roles, advisory work, governance reviews, and reported enterprise experience. They do not describe specific organizations. Any resemblance to identifiable enterprises arises from the prevalence of the underlying patterns rather than from direct reference.

First edition, published in 2026.

Printed in the United States of America.

For the executives who knew something was wrong and could not yet name it.

“The purpose of a system is what it does.”

— Stafford Beer

“Moving from assisted to autonomous isn’t just a technology decision. It’s a governance one.”

— ServiceNow, Enterprise AI Maturity Index 2026

CONTENTS

How to Read This Book

Reading roadmaps for different audiences

This book is structured to reward both linear reading and selective reading. The chapters build on each other, but the framework is designed so that an executive who reads selectively can still extract a coherent argument. The following roadmaps suggest reading orders calibrated to the time available and the position the reader holds.

IF YOU ARE THE CEO OR A BOARD MEMBER

Three hours

Introduction → Chapter 3 → Chapter 11 → Chapter 13 → Chapter 15 → Conclusion

These chapters carry the central thesis. You will understand why governance is the variable that distinguishes the Pacesetter cohort, what the keystone is, what the diagnostic patterns reveal, and what the sequenced work involves. The remainder of the book is the substantiation, which you can defer to your team or read selectively.

IF YOU ARE THE CIO

Six to eight hours

Introduction → Chapters 1, 2, 4 → Chapters 9 and 11 → Chapter 13 → Part Four → Conclusion

This is the longest of the executive paths because it covers the territory the CIO is uniquely responsible for. Chapters 1 and 2 explain why conventional governance is mismatched to the technology now in production. Chapter 4 introduces the framework. Chapter 9 (AI Use and Lifecycle Governance) and Chapter 11 (Decision Rights) cover the two dimensions where CIO authority is most directly tested. Chapter 13 names the patterns that recur across CIO portfolios. Part Four is the work itself — sequencing, phases, and the keystone principle. If your time is shorter, read Chapters 4, 9, 11, and 16, in that order.

IF YOU ARE THE CRO, CISO, OR GENERAL COUNSEL

Five to six hours

Introduction → Part One → Chapters 4 and 11 → Part Three → Chapter 15 → Conclusion

Read the dimension chapters most relevant to your portfolio: 5–6 for the General Counsel; 6, 7, 10 for the CRO; 7, 8, 10 for the CISO. The patterns in Part Three will help you recognize the operating condition in your own organization.

IF YOU ARE THE CHIEF AUDIT EXECUTIVE OR THE ASSESSOR

The whole book

Read in order

The framework's analytical structure depends on the sequence the chapters develop. The dimension chapters in Part Two establish the questions, Part Three explains how the patterns emerge, and Part Four describes the remediation logic. Skipping ahead diminishes the diagnostic discipline.

IF YOU ARE EVALUATING WHETHER TO ENGAGE EXTERNAL HELP

Two evenings

Introduction → Chapter 4 → Chapter 12 → Chapter 14 → Conclusion

Chapter 4 introduces the framework's structure. Chapter 12 explains the signature element that makes the assessment diagnostically valuable. Chapter 14 explains what self-assessment can do and what it cannot. You will know enough to scope an engagement appropriately.

INTRODUCTION

The Gap Between What We Built and What We Govern

"Governance is what makes the difference between what an organization formally is and what it actually does."
— Charles Handy

The kind of meeting that prompted this book has taken place, in one variation or another, across multiple engagements over the past several years. The composite that follows draws on those engagements; the specifics have been changed but the shape has not. Picture a large financial services firm that has invested heavily in AI governance over the prior eighteen months. There is a committee. There is a policy. There is an inventory of approved AI use cases. There are quarterly reports to the audit committee. By the standard of what most enterprises had stood up by late 2024, the firm is ahead of its peers.

The conversation that surfaces the gap typically unfolds something like this. The Chief Risk Officer — an experienced executive, with the calm manner of someone who has been through several regulatory cycles — is walking through the AI inventory. The spreadsheet lists, say, forty-seven approved AI use cases.

"How complete is this?" the reviewer asks.

She pauses. "For what we know about, it is complete."

"What do you not know about?"

Another pause, longer this time. "We enabled Microsoft Copilot for the firm eight months ago. It is being used in legal, in finance, in HR. We did not put it on this list because it did not feel like a new AI deployment. It was a feature of software we already had. Salesforce turned on Einstein in our sales cloud sometime last year. ServiceNow turned on Now Assist for our IT service desk. None of those are on the list either."

"So what is the actual scope of AI operating in the firm?"

She looks at the spreadsheet for a long moment. "I think," she says carefully, "it is somewhere between two and five times what is on this list. I can't tell you which end of that range."

And there the conversation sits. The board will be expecting a status report in six weeks. She has a forty- seven-item AI inventory. The firm has perhaps two hundred AI capabilities operating. The committee she chairs has been governing the forty-seven and has no governance over the rest. The forty-seven are the ones that passed through formal approval. The remainder appeared through software activations that no one had thought to bring to the committee, because the vendors that provided them were not new vendors and the activations had not felt like new deployments.

This is a moment that has, in one form or another, recurred across the kinds of organizations the framework was built to study. The specifics vary. The shape does not. A serious executive, doing serious work, discovers that the governance she is responsible for is operating over a fraction of what it nominally addresses. The discovery is uncomfortable. The discovery is also the beginning of the work.

This book is about that work.

THE LINE THAT WAS CROSSED

Sometime in the last three years, the enterprises I work with crossed a line. I cannot tell you exactly when. Few of them can either.

Before the line, enterprise technology was something you bought, deployed, and supervised. People made decisions. Software helped them make those decisions faster, with better information. The supervision model assumed a human stayed in the loop, in the chair, accountable for the consequences.

After the line, that model began to come apart. Not all at once. Not in any way anyone announced. The unraveling happened in places no one was looking. A customer service workflow that used to route exceptions to a manager now routes them to a model. A vendor screening process that used to require a human to read the security questionnaire now uses an AI to summarize it. A risk register that used to be updated by an analyst now ingests signals from a continuous monitoring tool and updates itself.

Each individual change was small. None was wrong, exactly. Each improved some metric — speed, throughput, cost — that the organization had explicitly asked someone to improve. The aggregate of these changes did something the organization had never asked anyone to do. It replaced a system of human-accountable decisions with a system of algorithmic decisions for which accountability had not been redesigned.

Most enterprises are now operating this system without a functioning governance layer over it. They do not know which decisions their models are making, at what frequency, on whose behalf, under what authority. They have policies that prohibit some uses of AI. They lack the mechanisms to detect when those policies are being violated. They have inventories of AI systems that, as the CRO in the windowless room discovered, are incomplete by orders of magnitude. They have AI governance committees that meet quarterly and review documentation prepared for those meetings, while the systems the committees nominally govern make millions of consequential decisions in the intervals between.

Governance fit for the autonomous enterprise is not built by extending what already exists. It is built by recognizing what already exists has been quietly outflanked.

This is the gap. This book is about how it got here, what shape it takes, and what to do about it.

HOW I CAME TO THIS WORK

I spent the better part of two decades inside enterprise technology and governance, including service as a Chief Information Officer. Across those years, I helped build the artifacts this book is, in part, an indictment of. I authored policies. I commissioned controls. I chaired governance committees. I sat through audit committee briefings and produced documentation the audit committees were satisfied to receive. Later, in other executive roles, I also read those artifacts from the other side of the table — as someone trying to figure out what they actually said about the operational reality of the organization. Neither vantage point gave me much satisfaction with the state of the discipline.

Some of the organizations I worked with were sophisticated about governance. Many were not. The sophisticated ones were sophisticated in a particular way. They had good documentation, defensible audits, and the ability to produce evidence of governance when asked. What they generally did not have, and what I have not yet encountered in fully developed form, was governance that reliably produced the outcomes governance is supposed to produce.

Governance is supposed to reduce risk. It is supposed to ensure that the decisions an organization makes are made by people authorized to make them, with the information necessary to make them well, accountable to other people who can intervene when those decisions go wrong. It is supposed to be a system that learns. A system that responds to evidence of its own failure by changing how it works.

Most enterprise governance functions do not do these things in any reliable way. They produce artifacts. They satisfy auditors. They generate documentation. The artifacts and documentation are real. The underlying governance is, at many firms, performative.

This was a manageable problem when the decisions being governed were slow, visible, and made by identifiable humans. A defective governance system was still better than no governance system at all. The imperfections were absorbed by the humans in the loop, who applied judgment when the formal process broke down.

It is not a manageable problem anymore. The decisions are now fast, often invisible, and made increasingly by systems whose decision-making nobody in the organization can fully audit. The humans who used to absorb imperfections in the governance process are no longer in the loop. The imperfections are now structural exposures.

WHAT THIS BOOK IS

This book lays out a framework. The framework has a name — the Integrated Risk and AI Governance Maturity Model — that is more bureaucratic than the framework itself. At its heart, it is an instrument for honest self-assessment by enterprises that have begun to suspect something is wrong with how they govern and cannot yet name what it is.

The framework has seven dimensions, organized on a five-stage maturity scale. It surfaces specific findings about an enterprise's governance condition in ways that ordinary assessments do not. The most useful findings come not from any single dimension but from patterns the dimensions make in aggregate.

Across the work that informs this framework, four cumulative patterns have come to seem to me the most important diagnoses an enterprise can receive about its own governance. The patterns have names: Documentation Theater, Locked-In, Unmodeled, Misaligned. Each describes a specific structural condition that, once named, becomes difficult to ignore.

This book teaches what the patterns are, how to recognize them in your own organization, and what to do about them. It is intended as a practical instrument for executives — CIOs, CROs, general counsels, chief audit executives, and the board members who oversee them — who suspect their governance is not where it needs to be and who want a defensible way to articulate the gap and a coherent plan for closing it.

WHAT THIS BOOK IS NOT

This book is not a manual for building an AI governance program from nothing. There are competent treatments of that work, some of them quite good. What I want to do here is something different. I want to show why the AI governance programs built in most enterprises over the past three years are insufficient. And why the insufficiency is structural rather than incidental.

Nor is this a technical treatment. There are no architectural diagrams of model risk management infrastructure, no detailed walkthroughs of monitoring instrumentation, no vendor comparisons. The level of analysis is executive. The audience is the people whose job is to know whether the governance is working, not the people whose job is to build it.

Finally, this book takes positions. It does so because governance failures are rarely corrected by language that is too cautious to name them. I have tried to be fair, but I have not tried to be bland. The executives this book is written for do not need reassurance. They need a clearer way to see the gap between the governance they have documented and the governance their enterprises actually operate.

A NOTE ON THE ANECDOTES

Throughout this book, I have included case studies and illustrative scenes. The conversation with the CRO that opens this introduction is one of them. These are not literal transcripts of specific engagements. They are composites, drawn from patterns observed across executive roles, advisory work, governance reviews, and reported enterprise experience. The CRO in the windowless room is not a specific person. The conversation I describe is not a specific conversation. The scene is true to a kind of moment that has occurred more times than I can count, with details adjusted to protect the confidentiality that advisory work depends on.

I take this approach for two reasons. The first is professional. The work I do is conducted under terms that prohibit attribution. The second is intellectual. The patterns this book is about are not specific to any one firm. They are general. The anecdotes are constructed to illustrate the general patterns rather than to report on particular instances. The reader who recognizes themselves in a scene is not reading about themselves. They are reading about a pattern that has appeared in their firm and in many others.

A finding that is comfortable to receive is, in most cases, not telling the organization anything it did not already know.

THE STAKES

The state of enterprise governance is more precarious than its operators have generally acknowledged. The pressure that autonomous AI is now placing on that governance is greater than the AI market has generally priced in. The next two years are likely to make the gap visible to boards, regulators, and shareholders. The organizations that have done the work will be ready for the conversation. The organizations that have not will conduct it under conditions of their choosing or under conditions imposed by events.

The clearest external evidence of this is ServiceNow's 2026 Enterprise AI Maturity Index, which identified a Pacesetter cohort — roughly one in five of the enterprises surveyed — materially ahead in AI maturity and in realizing value from AI investments. The remaining four in five were behind. The variable, ServiceNow found, was not budget or industry. It was orchestration, connected data, and governance built before deployment rather than after. Chapter 3 takes up what this divergence means and why it is widening.

The differential is not stable. It is compounding. Each year that the Pacesetters operate the governance infrastructure they have built, they realize returns that fund further capability. The further capability produces further returns. The non-Pacesetters are also investing, but their investments produce partial returns that fund partial capability that produces further partial returns. Over five years, the gap widens to a point that, in some industries, it is becoming structural.

This book is for the executives who want to close the gap before it closes on them. The work begins on the next page.

◆ ◆ ◆

A practical note before you proceed. The structure of this book is designed to support both linear reading and selective reading. If you have read the roadmap on the prior pages and selected an entry point, follow it. If you want the full argument, read in order. Either way, the framework will reward the attention you give it. The deeper you go, the more diagnostic value it produces. The more diagnostic value it produces, the more honest the conversation it enables. The honest conversation is, in the end, the precondition for everything else.

PART ONE

The Problem

How enterprise governance arrived at its present condition, why autonomous AI is structurally different from prior waves of technology, and what separates the organizations realizing AI returns from those that are not.

CHAPTER I

The Decade Governance Lost

"Only the paranoid survive. There is at least one point in the history of any company when you have to change dramatically to rise to the next level of performance. Miss that moment — and you start to decline."
— Andrew Grove

Sometime around 2015, enterprise governance entered a quiet crisis that almost no one named at the time. The crisis was not that governance was being attacked. The crisis was that the technology landscape governance was supposed to govern had begun changing faster than governance could keep up with. The gap between the two was widening every year.

By 2020, the gap was wide enough that careful observers had begun to notice. By 2023, it was wide enough that incidents began surfacing in public ways. Model outputs that embarrassed firms. AI deployments that produced regulatory inquiries. Vendor changes that exposed dependencies the customer organizations did not know they had. By 2025, the gap had become structural. Enterprises were no longer trying to close it. They were trying to manage its consequences.

This chapter is about how the gap opened. The story is not one of negligence. The people who built enterprise governance over the past three decades were serious professionals working competently within the constraints they faced. The story is one of mismatch. Governance models designed for one era of technology met the realities of a quite different era and could not adapt. Understanding the mismatch is the prerequisite for fixing it. Skipping the diagnosis goes badly.

THE ERA GOVERNANCE WAS DESIGNED FOR

Enterprise governance, as large organizations practice it, was substantially formalized between the late 1990s and the late 2000s. The catalysts were specific. Sarbanes-Oxley after the accounting scandals of the early 2000s. Basel II for financial institutions. HIPAA for healthcare. PCI for retailers handling payment data. Each of these regulatory regimes assumed a particular shape of risk and prescribed a particular shape of response.

The assumed shape of risk was institutional and slow-moving. Risks emerged from human decisions, organizational processes, and infrastructure investments that took months or years to mature. The response was a governance machinery built around documentation, periodic review, defined approval thresholds, and audit-defensible evidence trails. The machinery was designed to be examined retrospectively, by auditors, by regulators, by litigators, and to demonstrate after the fact that the organization had taken reasonable care.

Within that paradigm, governance worked well enough. Not perfectly. There were gaps, abuses, and predictable failures. But the model was coherent. It assumed humans made the decisions that mattered. It assumed those humans were identifiable and accountable. It assumed the decisions could be reconstructed and examined. And it assumed the volume of consequential decisions was small enough for governance attention to be allocated to them deliberately.

Every one of those assumptions has been undermined by the technology that has entered the enterprise since then.

THE SLOW EROSION OF THE FIRST ASSUMPTION

The first assumption was that humans made the consequential decisions. As recently as fifteen years ago this was substantially true even for organizations that had heavily invested in automation. The automation moved data, generated reports, executed defined steps in workflows. The decisions, properly understood, remained human. A loan officer approved the loan. A claims adjuster paid the claim. A buyer authorized the purchase. The software accelerated and informed; it did not decide.

This assumption began to erode with rules-based automation in the 2010s. Decision engines for credit scoring, fraud detection, and underwriting began making categorical decisions at volumes humans could not have reviewed individually. Accept. Deny. Refer. The decisions were governed by approving the rules, not by approving each decision. A governance committee would approve a rule that said "deny credit applications below score X." The rule would then make millions of decisions consistent with that approval, none of which received individual review.

This was workable, in part, because the rules were explicable. A loan officer could reconstruct why a decision was made. The rule said so. The rule could be audited, debated, and changed. Accountability for the decision flowed back to the people who had authorized the rule.

Machine learning systems began entering the enterprise in volume around 2015 and accelerated through the 2020s. Where rules-based systems had been transparent (anyone could read the rule), machine learning systems were probabilistic. The decision was a function of weights and patterns derived from training data, not of an articulable rule. Two equivalent applications could receive different decisions, and the difference could not always be reconstructed in terms a human could meaningfully evaluate.

Governance frameworks largely did not adapt. Firms applied the same governance posture to machine learning systems that they had applied to rules-based systems. Approve the model, then let the model decide. The fact that the model's decisions could not be reconstructed in the same way was, at most firms, simply not addressed. The audit committees received documentation about model approval. What the model did after approval was not part of the audit conversation.

THE EROSION OF THE SECOND ASSUMPTION

The second assumption was that the humans responsible for decisions were identifiable and accountable. As long as decisions were made by named humans, this was self-evident. The decision- maker's name was on the document. Their signature was on the approval. Their identity was traceable through the workflow. If the decision was wrong, the person who made it could be located, asked, and held accountable.

The first erosion came not from AI but from the rise of platform-mediated decisions. As enterprises moved decision workflows onto platforms (first email and document systems, then collaboration tools, then dedicated workflow platforms), the platforms began to absorb some of the decision-making. A document was routed through a workflow defined years earlier by someone who had since left the firm. The workflow approved certain things automatically and escalated others. The people approving at each stage often had no individual judgment about the substantive content of the decision. Only about whether it conformed to the criteria the workflow had been built around. Accountability became diffuse. The CEO had approved the policy. The workflow had been built by IT. The platform vendor had configured the workflow. The person clicking "approve" was applying a rule someone else had set.

The second erosion came from AI. As AI systems began making consequential decisions, the question of accountability sharpened. If a customer service AI tells a customer they are not eligible for a refund, and the customer was in fact eligible, who is accountable? The data scientist who trained the model? The product manager who deployed it? The vendor who provided the underlying model? The executive who authorized the deployment? In practice, accountability has typically been distributed among everyone and concentrated on no one.

Governance frameworks still ask: who decided. They get answers that do not actually identify a decision-maker. They accept the answers because they have no better alternative.

THE EROSION OF THE THIRD ASSUMPTION

The third assumption was that consequential decisions could be reconstructed and examined. This is the assumption auditability rested on. If a decision turned out to be wrong, the reasoning behind it could be retrieved and evaluated.

Machine learning systems undermined this assumption mechanically. A model's decision can be reconstructed in the sense that the inputs can be retrieved and the output recomputed. It cannot be reconstructed in the sense that the human meaning of the decision can be articulated. "The model assigned a probability of 0.73" is not the same kind of explanation as "the loan officer denied the loan because the applicant's debt-to-income ratio was above the threshold."

Generative AI made this worse. A large language model can produce different outputs to identical inputs, depending on the random seed and the temperature setting. The output cannot be reconstructed precisely. The reasoning behind any particular output cannot be examined in terms an auditor would find acceptable. The system's behavior can change substantially when the underlying model is updated by the vendor, often without notice.

Governance frameworks have not, by and large, absorbed the implications of this. They still ask for audit trails. They still expect full explainability of individual decisions. They still treat partial or unavailable explanation as a deficiency to be corrected, rather than as a structural feature of the technology that requires governance to be rethought from a different starting point.

THE EROSION OF THE FOURTH ASSUMPTION

The fourth assumption was that the volume of consequential decisions was small enough for governance attention to be allocated deliberately. This is, in many ways, the most important assumption, and the one most thoroughly destroyed by autonomous AI.

A risk committee that meets quarterly can review, perhaps, two dozen significant decisions in a year. A board risk committee can review fewer. The governance model assumes this is enough. It assumes the consequential decisions number in the dozens or perhaps the hundreds per year, and that the rest of the organizational decision-making consists of routine matters that need not be governed individually.

An autonomous AI agent can make hundreds of thousands of decisions in a day. Each one, individually, might be small. Each one might also be consequential in some context. A customer-facing chatbot promising something it should not have promised. A procurement agent placing an order with a vendor not on the approved list. A pricing engine setting a price that exposes the firm to regulatory liability. None of these crosses the threshold for board review individually. The aggregate exposure may cross it many times over before any single decision is examined.

Governance models designed for hundreds of consequential decisions per year are quietly broken by systems making millions of decisions per day. The framework looks intact because no single decision crosses a review threshold. The framework is in fact bypassed because nothing aggregates the small decisions into a view of cumulative exposure.

WHY NO ONE NOTICED

This was a slow erosion, conducted in pieces, by people who in most cases did not understand that they were eroding anything. The data scientists who built the models did not see themselves as redesigning governance. The product managers who deployed them did not see themselves as bypassing controls. The auditors who reviewed the deployments did not see themselves as accepting a degraded standard. Each transaction looked locally reasonable. The aggregate transaction was that governance had been substantially rebuilt around technologies it was not designed for, without anyone signing off on the rebuild.

Why did the people who should have noticed not notice?

Several reasons. The first is that governance is, at most enterprises, a defensive function. It produces audit-defensibility, regulatory compliance, board reporting. It does not, typically, originate strategic direction. The strategic direction across the past decade has come from the technology side. From CIOs and CTOs pursuing digital transformation. From chief data officers building data programs. From business unit leaders demanding AI capabilities. Governance has been positioned to follow, not lead. When the lead direction is moving faster than governance can adapt to, the gap opens. Governance does not have the standing to slow the lead direction down.

The second is that governance maturity is genuinely hard to measure. A firm with a well-documented control program, a thorough policy library, a current risk register, and a functioning audit committee can plausibly claim to be governed well. The evidence that it is not — that the controls do not actually mitigate the risks the firm faces, that the policies do not bind behavior, that the risk register is decorative — requires the kind of triangulated, multi-source assessment that ordinary audits do not produce. Few firms have ever received such an assessment. They do not know what they do not know.

The third is that the consequences of weak governance have been, until recently, slow to surface. Incidents happened, but they were isolated, attributable to specific failures, and remediated incrementally. The structural inadequacy of the underlying governance model was not visible in any single incident. It was visible only across many incidents over many years, viewed by someone with the perspective to recognize the pattern.

The fourth, and the one I want to emphasize, is that the technology landscape has been changing fast enough that any single governance team's view has been local. The team that worried about cloud governance was different from the team that worried about data governance, which was different from the team that worried about vendor governance, which was different from the team that worried about AI governance. Each team built its own framework, each addressing the specific concerns of its local domain. The cumulative effect of the fragmented frameworks — the absence of any single governance posture that addressed how the domains interacted — was nobody's specific responsibility. So it became nobody's specific concern.

WHERE WE ARE NOW

The current state, at most large enterprises, is the cumulative result of these slow erosions. Specifically:

Documented governance exists in volume. Firms can produce a thorough policy library, a risk register, a control catalog, an AI governance committee charter, a vendor risk management framework, and incident response playbooks. What that volume describes and what the organization actually does are, at many firms, two different things, and the difference has widened with AI.

Operational governance is uneven. Some functions operate as documented. Many do not. The gap between documentation and operation is, at most firms, larger than the executives who oversee the documentation realize. The gap is not generally caused by negligence. It is caused by the cumulative effect of decisions made over many years to defer the harder work of operational governance in favor of meeting more visible compliance demands.

AI governance, where it exists, is typically nascent. Most enterprises stood up some form of AI governance in 2023 or 2024, in response to public attention on generative AI. The governance was typically a committee, a policy, and an inventory. The committee meets infrequently. The policy is generic. The inventory is incomplete. None of the three reaches the actual decisions AI is making in the firm on a day-to-day basis.

Decision rights are, at most enterprises, the most consequentially weak component of the governance system. Decision rights frameworks were typically authored decades ago, encoded into workflows that have since calcified, and have rarely been revised in response to evidence. The frameworks address financial transactions, capital allocation, and a defined set of regulatory matters. They do not generally address the new categories of decisions AI has introduced: agent authorization, model update validation, autonomous action, AI-assisted customer engagement. Those decisions are governed informally or not at all.

This is the situation as I write. It is not stable. It is not, in the medium term, defensible. And it is not, given the pace at which AI is being deployed, sustainable for much longer.

THE DECADE AHEAD

The decade ahead will, I expect, force a reckoning with this. The reckoning will come from multiple directions at once.

Regulators will arrive. The EU AI Act is the most visible signal. National regulators in the United States, the United Kingdom, and elsewhere are likely to follow. The early implementations of these regulations will be flawed and inconsistent. The underlying direction is unambiguous. Enterprises will be required to demonstrate governance over AI in ways that they cannot currently demonstrate.

Boards will demand accountability. Board members who were comfortable taking a light-touch posture toward AI in 2024 will become uncomfortable as material incidents make AI governance a fiduciary topic rather than a technology topic. The boards will ask hard questions of executives. The executives without good answers will be replaced.

Insurers will tighten. The cyber insurance market began tightening five years ago in response to ransomware. The AI liability insurance market will tighten similarly in response to AI incidents. Firms that cannot demonstrate governance maturity will face higher premiums, larger deductibles, and narrower coverage.

Customers will demand transparency. Enterprise buyers will increasingly ask about AI governance in vendor due diligence. Consumer-facing firms will face questions about how AI is involved in decisions affecting customers.

The organizations that can answer credibly will gain trust. Those that cannot will lose business.

Each of these pressures is already visible, in early form, in the advisory work this framework is designed to support. None is at full force yet. All are moving in the same direction. The firms that have not begun the work of governance modernization will, within two to three years, find themselves trying to do in a panic what they could have done deliberately over a longer timeframe.

◆ ◆ ◆

The argument of this chapter has been historical. The argument of the next chapter is structural. AI is not a continuation of prior waves of technology. It is a different kind of thing, and the difference is what enterprise governance, designed for prior waves, cannot accommodate. Understanding what is different about it is the prerequisite for the framework that follows.

CHAPTER IN BRIEF

- Enterprise governance was formalized for institutional, slow-moving risk between the late 1990s and the late 2000s, under regimes like Sarbanes-Oxley, Basel II, HIPAA, and PCI.
- Four foundational assumptions of that model — human decision-makers, identifiable accountability, reconstructable reasoning, and small decision volume — have been undermined by the technology that has entered the enterprise since.
- The erosion happened slowly, in pieces, by people who did not see themselves as redesigning governance. Each local transaction looked reasonable. The aggregate transaction was a structural rebuilding that no one signed off on.
- The consequences are now arriving. Regulators, boards, insurers, and customers are all moving in the same direction. The window for deliberate work is open. It will not remain open indefinitely.

CHAPTER II

Why AI Breaks Governance

"The greatest danger in times of turbulence is not the turbulence; it is to act with yesterday's logic."
— Peter Drucker

AI is governed badly at most enterprises. This is not because the governance teams are weak. It is because AI has four properties that conventional governance frameworks were not designed to handle. The properties are not novel ideas. They are observable in the technology, visible in any honest assessment, and well understood by the AI practitioners who build and deploy these systems. They are not, however, well understood by most of the executives whose job is to govern them.

This chapter names the four properties. It explains why each breaks a conventional governance assumption. And it sets up the argument, developed in the rest of the book, that governance fit for AI requires structural redesign rather than incremental extension. Adding AI-specific policies to a conventional governance framework does not produce AI governance. It produces conventional governance with AI policies. The two are not the same.

PROPERTY ONE: SPEED

AI systems make decisions at machine speed. Not at the speed of the workflow that surrounds the decision. At the speed of the model itself. A model can evaluate a customer transaction in milliseconds, generate a response, and act on it before any human in the workflow is aware the transaction occurred. In aggregate, a deployed AI capability can make millions of such decisions in a day.

Governance frameworks were built for slower decision-making. They assume that consequential decisions take hours, days, or weeks to make. The assumption is encoded into the frameworks in specific ways. Approval workflows assume the decision will pause for human review. Risk evaluation assumes the risk will be evaluated before the decision is made. Audit logging assumes the audit will be available before any related decision needs to be made.

None of these assumptions holds for AI. The decision is made before the human review can occur. The risk is evaluated, if at all, after the decision has been acted on. The audit is produced after the fact, with the consequence of the decision already in motion. The framework continues to operate. The framework is also bypassed in the sense that matters most. The consequential decisions are made by the AI, on the AI's timing, with the framework reviewing after the fact.

The remediation is not to slow the AI down. AI that operates at human speed loses most of the value of being AI. The remediation is to redesign the framework to govern at AI speed. The redesign requires the framework to be operating before the AI is making decisions, not after. It requires the boundaries of the AI's authority to be defined in advance, with the AI operating within those boundaries unconditionally. It requires monitoring that operates at AI speed and produces alerts that pre-empt the framework rather than reporting to it after the fact.

Few enterprise governance frameworks have been redesigned this way. The frameworks still operate at human speed. The AI still operates at AI speed. The gap is filled, when it is filled at all, by ad-hoc arrangements that vary from use case to use case and from team to team.

PROPERTY TWO: OPACITY

AI systems make decisions whose reasoning cannot be reconstructed in human-meaningful terms. The output of a large language model is the result of attention patterns across billions of parameters, each of which contributes a small amount to the final result. The contribution of any individual parameter cannot be isolated. The reasoning, in the sense an auditor or regulator would mean the word, does not exist.

This is sometimes overstated. AI models can be interrogated. The interrogation produces something. What it produces, however, is not the explanation a human would produce. It is a model of what an explanation might look like, generated by the same kind of system that produced the original output, with no guarantee that the explanation accurately reflects the actual reasoning. The phrase "the model decided X because of Y" is, in most cases, generated by a process that does not have access to the actual computation that produced the original decision.

The accountable executive cannot defend the decision. She can only defend the system that produced the decision.

Governance frameworks rest on the assumption that decisions can be explained. The explanation is what makes accountability meaningful. The decision-maker can be held accountable for the decision because the decision can be examined, the reasoning can be evaluated, and the failure modes can be identified. Without the explanation, the accountability has no purchase. The decision-maker can be named, but the decision-maker cannot defend the decision in terms an auditor would find acceptable.

This is not, in the main, a technical limitation that further engineering will dissolve. It is, to a substantial degree, structural to how machine learning produces outputs. Some interpretability tools have improved; the structural condition has not changed materially. Governance frameworks that assume per-decision explainability will be available are governing against a model of the technology that does not match how the technology operates.

The remediation is to govern the system rather than the decision. The system is approved for specified use cases, within specified boundaries, with monitoring of outputs in aggregate rather than individually. The accountability is for the system's design, deployment, and operation, not for any specific decision. The shift is uncomfortable for governance functions accustomed to decision-level accountability. The shift is necessary because decision-level accountability is no longer available.

PROPERTY THREE: SCALE

AI systems operate at scale that overwhelms human review. A single deployed model can make millions of decisions in a day. A vendor providing a foundation model serves thousands of customer organizations, each of which is using the model in dozens or hundreds of distinct ways. The aggregate decision volume of the AI deployed in a large enterprise is comparable to the aggregate decision volume of the entire human workforce.

Governance frameworks were not designed for this volume. They assume that consequential decisions can be reviewed individually, escalated when warranted, and aggregated periodically. The assumption is workable at human decision volume. At AI decision volume, it produces governance that is, at most, sampling the decisions being made. The governance reviews a small percentage of decisions and infers from the sample about the rest. The inference is statistically reasonable. It is also fundamentally different from the decision-by-decision governance the framework was built to provide.

Scale also produces concentration. A single foundation model failure affects every customer using it. A single AI vendor outage cascades across every business process that depends on the vendor's capability. A single fine-tuning error affects every output of the deployed model until the error is identified and corrected. The concentration of consequence is unprecedented in enterprise technology. The closest analog is the concentration that emerged with cloud computing in the 2010s, and the AI concentration is, in some ways, more acute.

Governance frameworks have not generally absorbed the concentration risk. They treat AI vendors as one category of vendor among many, with the same vendor risk methodology applied. The methodology was built for vendors whose failure modes are localized. AI vendor failure modes are not localized. They cascade. The methodology has to be extended for this, and few enterprises have extended it.

PROPERTY FOUR: MUTABILITY

AI systems change behavior over time without explicit redeployment. Three mechanisms produce this. The first is vendor-driven updates. The vendor retrains or fine-tunes the underlying model and pushes the updated version to all customers, often with limited notification. The second is the operation of fine- tuning by the customer organization itself, when the firm retrains the model on its own data. The third is the operation of the model's own ongoing learning, when the model is configured to learn from operational feedback during deployment.

Conventional governance frameworks assume the systems being governed are stable. The framework approves a system, the system operates as approved, and the framework reapproves periodically. The reapproval assumes the system has not materially changed in the interim. For AI, this assumption fails routinely. The system is materially changing on a continuous basis. The approval given six months ago may be approving a system that no longer exists in the form that was approved.

The remediation is to govern the mutability rather than the static system. The framework specifies the conditions under which the system can change without re-approval, the conditions that require re- approval, the monitoring that detects when changes have occurred, and the response when changes are detected. The framework is, in effect, governing a process of continuous change rather than a stable artifact. Few governance functions have made this transition. They are still governing as if the systems were stable.

THE FOUR PROPERTIES TOGETHER

Each of the four properties individually stresses governance. The combination is where conventional governance loses its purchase. AI is fast and opaque and scaled and mutable. A framework that can govern any one of these properties separately may not be able to govern all four together. The interactions amplify the difficulties.

Consider an autonomous AI agent that takes actions on the firm's behalf. The agent operates at machine speed, so the conventional approval workflow cannot keep up. The agent's actions cannot be reconstructed in human-meaningful terms, so the accountability is for the agent's design rather than for the specific actions. The agent operates at scale, so the actions cannot be reviewed individually. And the agent's behavior changes over time, so the approval given at deployment may no longer apply to the current behavior.

Each of the four properties is now present at the same time. The conventional governance framework can address some of them. It cannot, in its current form, address all of them simultaneously. The agent is, in practice, ungoverned. It is operating within a governance framework that was not built for it and cannot be made to govern it without redesign.

This is why AI governance, at most enterprises, is failing to govern AI. The frameworks were not built for it. The frameworks have been extended for it. The extension is insufficient. The redesign required has not been undertaken.

◆ ◆ ◆

The next chapter describes the divergence in outcomes that this gap is producing. Some organizations have closed the gap. Most have not. The cumulative consequence of the difference between the two is what makes the next two years the most important window for enterprise governance in the past two decades.

CHAPTER IN BRIEF

- AI has four properties that conventional governance was not built to handle: speed, opacity, scale, and mutability. Each individually stresses a foundational assumption of governance. The combination is where conventional governance loses its purchase.
- Speed strains approval workflows that depend on human review. Opacity strains accountability that depends on explainable reasoning. Scale strains sampling-based oversight. Mutability strains periodic re-approval based on stable system behavior.
- The remediation is not to slow AI down. The remediation is structural redesign: govern the system rather than the decision, define boundaries in advance, monitor at machine speed, and treat continuous change as the default condition rather than the exception.
- Adding AI-specific policies to a conventional framework does not produce AI governance. It produces conventional governance with AI policies. The two are not the same.

CHAPTER III

The Pacesetter Divergence

"The strategy of the winners has always been to win the war before the battle."

— Sun Tzu, paraphrased by Geoffrey Moore

In its 2025 and 2026 Enterprise AI Maturity Indices, ServiceNow published research that is, in my reading, among the more analytically useful work the enterprise AI industry has produced on the question of differential outcomes. The research surveyed thousands of executives about their AI deployments, the practices distinguishing them, and the value being realized from AI. The headline finding was numerical and uncomfortable. Roughly one in five enterprises was materially ahead — in maturity across the pillars ServiceNow measured and in realizing value from AI investments. The remaining four in five were behind.

ServiceNow called this leading group the Pacesetters. The term is apt, and this book adopts it for convenience; the framework that follows in Parts Two through Four is independent of the term, and its diagnostic vocabulary stands on its own analytical ground. The Pacesetters were not just ahead on a maturity index. They were setting the pace that the rest of the cohort was trying to follow. The remaining majority were investing at comparable levels, deploying comparable technology, working with comparable vendors. They were producing different outcomes.

The research was not the first to identify the divergence. It was the first to quantify it. Earlier research had suggested that enterprise AI investments were producing variable returns. The variability had been treated, in the discourse, as a function of execution quality. Some enterprises were executing well. Some were executing badly. The implied remediation was better execution.

The ServiceNow research surfaced something different. The Pacesetters and the rest of the cohort were not separated by execution quality. They were separated by the governance infrastructure each had built. The research identifies governance infrastructure as one of the defining characteristics of the Pacesetter cohort. The framing in this book — that the governance infrastructure is the proximate cause of the differential returns — goes a step beyond what the research itself claims, and reflects the author's interpretation rather than ServiceNow's published conclusion.

This chapter is about the divergence the research describes, the governance infrastructure that produces it, and why the next two to three years are the window in which the divergence becomes structural. Firms that close the gap in this window can still close it. Firms that do not close it in this window will, in my judgment, find the gap difficult to close at all.

WHAT THE PACESETTERS HAVE THAT OTHERS DO NOT

The Pacesetters share a set of characteristics that the rest of the cohort does not. The characteristics are not, primarily, technology characteristics. The Pacesetters are not using better models. They are not, on average, larger or better-funded than their peers. They are not concentrated in any single industry. They are distinguished by their governance practices.

Pacesetter organizations had aligned executive understanding. The CEO, the CRO, the CIO, the General Counsel, and the chief audit executive had spent the time required to develop a shared view of what AI governance was supposed to produce, what risks it was supposed to mitigate, and how success would be measured. They did not all agree on the details, but they were aligned on the substance.

Pacesetter organizations had operational governance that was actually operating. The committees met regularly and reviewed substantive findings. The policies were enforced through workflows that detected violations and escalated them. The risk registers were current and informed actual decisions. The vendor assessments were rigorous and produced consequential outcomes including, occasionally, vendor termination. The AI inventories were complete and used as the basis for prioritization.

Pacesetter organizations had learning systems that converted evidence into structural change. Incidents produced post-incident reviews that produced recommendations that were actually implemented. Audit findings produced remediation that addressed root causes rather than surface symptoms. Vendor failures produced updates to the vendor risk methodology. AI behavior anomalies produced updates to the AI governance framework. The systems were not just operating; they were improving.

Pacesetter organizations had decision rights that had been deliberately redesigned for AI. The authority matrix had been extended to cover AI-specific decision categories. The matrix was encoded into the workflows that routed decisions in practice. The named decision-makers understood their decision authority and exercised it. The accountability for AI decisions was, in fact, identifiable, even when the conventional explainability standards were not met.

Each of these characteristics requires time, executive attention, and political work to build. The Pacesetters had begun the work earlier, typically in 2022 or 2023. The non-Pacesetters had typically begun the work later, or had begun it nominally without committing to the political work it requires. By 2026, the cumulative effect of two to three years of governance work was producing the differential the research identified.

The Pacesetters were not, primarily, executing better. They were doing different work.

THE COMPOUND EFFECT

The differential is not stable. It is compounding. Each year that the Pacesetters operate the governance infrastructure they have built, they realize returns that are reinvested in further capability. The further capability produces further returns. The further returns are reinvested. The cycle is what produces the Pacesetter lead.

The non-Pacesetters are not standing still. They are also investing. The investments are, however, partial. They are producing partial returns. The partial returns are reinvested in further partial capability. The partial capability produces further partial returns. The cycle produces growth, but at a slower rate than the Pacesetter cycle. The gap widens.

This is the mechanism by which competitive position deteriorates slowly. No single quarter shows a dramatic shortfall. The trajectory, viewed over five years, is unmistakable. The firm that was indistinguishable from its leading competitor in 2024 is, in 2029, several years behind. The lag, once established, is difficult to close. The leading competitor has continued to extend the lead during the years it took to recognize and respond to it.

In some industries, the compound effect has already produced visible market consequences. Companies that did the governance work early are taking share from companies that did not. Companies that did the work are commanding premium valuations. Companies that did not are being acquired at discounts, or are being broken up, or are being replaced in their markets by competitors that grew faster than they did.

The compound effect is what makes the next two to three years consequential. The Pacesetter lead is currently substantial but recoverable. Firms that begin the governance work in 2026 can, by 2028, have closed most of the gap. Firms that begin in 2027 will have less time and a wider gap to close. Firms that have not begun by 2028 will, in my judgment, be unable to close the gap before the compound effect makes the competitive position structural.

CASE IN POINT

TWO INSURERS, IDENTICAL SPEND, DIVERGENT OUTCOMES

Two regional property and casualty insurers, headquartered within forty miles of each other, began enterprise AI programs within ninety days of one another in the autumn of 2022. Both were profitable. Both had similar revenue bands. Both had recently appointed Chief Data Officers. Their three--year AI investments differed by less than seven percent.

The figures in this case are illustrative composites, calibrated to reflect observed enterprise patterns rather than the financials of any specific organization.

The first insurer, which I will call North Atlantic Mutual, spent twelve months on what its CEO described as "the unglamorous work." The board chartered a governance committee with explicit authority to approve and to prohibit AI use cases. The decision rights matrix was extended to cover seven new categories of AI decisions before the first model went into production. The CRO and the General Counsel co-led the work. The first eighteen months produced no customer-facing AI capability. They produced governance.

The second insurer, which I will call Mid-Coast Insurance, moved faster. The CEO announced an AI strategy at an industry conference in early 2023. Customer-facing models were in pilot by mid-2023. By the end of that year, the firm had deployed a claims triage model, an underwriting assistant, and a chatbot for first-notice-of- loss. The governance committee existed on paper. It met twice that first year.

By the end of 2025, North Atlantic Mutual had eleven AI capabilities in production, all governed, all monitored, with documented decommissioning processes already exercised on two early models that had not produced their projected lift. Underwriting time was down twenty-eight percent. Loss ratios had improved by 1.4 points. Mid-Coast had thirty-four AI capabilities running, sixteen of which were not in any inventory the firm could produce when its state regulator requested one. A class action over the claims triage model had been settled for nineteen million dollars. The firm was on its third Chief Data Officer.

Their AI spend across the three years had been within seven percent of each other. Their outcomes were not comparable. The variable was not investment level. The variable was the governance work the first firm did before the technology work and that the second firm did not.

WHY THE GAP PERSISTS

If the governance work is identifiable, the methodology is available, and the consequences of not doing it are visible, why has the gap persisted? Why is the cohort behind the Pacesetters still behind?

Several reasons. The first is that the governance work does not feel urgent. The AI investments are producing some returns, even if not the returns the Pacesetters realize. The partial returns are sufficient to satisfy short-term reporting demands. The deeper work that would produce the Pacesetter-level returns requires investment now in capability that will pay off later. The deferral is, locally, rational. It is also, cumulatively, what produces the persistent gap.

The second is that the governance work is uncomfortable. It involves the surfacing of dysfunction that has been comfortable for some executives to leave unsurfaced. It involves the modification of decision authority that some executives have been pleased to have. It involves the acknowledgment of investments that have not produced the returns they were sold as producing. Each of these elements requires political capital. Many firms have not been willing to spend it.

The third is that the governance work has been described, in the discourse, in ways that obscure its importance. The work has been presented as compliance overhead, as risk management housekeeping, as AI ethics. Each of these framings is partial and incidentally true. None captures the work's actual function, which is the construction of the infrastructure that makes AI investments productive. The framing problem has hidden the work's importance from the executives whose decision it is to undertake it.

The fourth is that the governance work takes longer to produce visible returns than other AI investments. A pilot AI deployment produces visible activity within weeks. A governance program reaches its operating state within twelve to eighteen months and its mature state within twenty-four to thirty-six. The activity bias of executive attention favors the pilot. The cumulative returns favor the governance. The non-Pacesetter cohort has allocated its attention in proportion to the activity rather than to the returns.

THE WINDOW

The window for closing the gap is open now. It will not, in my judgment, remain open indefinitely. Three forces are closing it.

The first is the maturation of the Pacesetter lead. The longer the Pacesetters operate their governance infrastructure, the further ahead they get. At some point, the lead becomes structural rather than recoverable. The point is not precise, but it is, in the industries I observe most closely, approximately three to five years out from the present. Firms that have not begun the work by then will find the gap difficult to close at all.

The second is the regulatory tightening that is now under way. The EU AI Act is in force. NIST AI RMF has been adopted. ISO 42001 is being implemented. The US regulatory environment is moving in similar directions, more slowly and less prescriptively but in the same direction. Firms that have not done the governance work will, increasingly, face regulatory consequences that the Pacesetters will not face. The consequences will further widen the operational gap.

The third is the maturation of insurance and contractual markets. Cyber insurance has been tightening for five years in response to ransomware. AI liability insurance will tighten similarly. Customer contractual demands for AI governance demonstration will sharpen. Vendor due diligence will become more rigorous. Each of these market mechanisms will reward the Pacesetters and penalize the rest of the cohort. The penalties will widen the financial gap. The widening will further entrench the Pacesetter position.

None of these forces is hypothetical. All are visible, in early form, in 2026. All will intensify over the next two to three years. The window is open now. It will not remain open indefinitely.

◆ ◆ ◆

The next chapter introduces the framework that this book is about. The framework is the instrument by which an organization can determine its current position relative to the Pacesetter cohort and identify the work required to close the gap. The instrument has seven dimensions and five maturity stages. Chapter 4 explains how they fit together.

CHAPTER IN BRIEF

- ServiceNow's 2025 and 2026 Enterprise AI Maturity Indices quantified what many practitioners had been observing: a Pacesetter cohort of roughly one in five enterprises is materially ahead in AI maturity and value realization; the remainder of the cohort is behind. ServiceNow defines the cohort not by budget or industry, but by orchestration, connected data, and governance built before deployment rather than after. The framework this book develops treats governance as the binding constraint among the three.
- The Pacesetters share four characteristics: aligned executive understanding, operational governance that is actually operating, learning systems that convert evidence into structural change, and decision rights deliberately redesigned for AI.
- The differential compounds annually. The gap widens. Firms that have not begun the work by 2028 will find the gap structural rather than recoverable.
- Three forces are closing the window: the maturing Pacesetter lead, regulatory tightening, and the hardening of insurance and contractual markets. The window is open in 2026. It will not remain open indefinitely.

PART TWO

The Framework

Seven dimensions, five stages, and the structural logic that holds them together.

CHAPTER IV

Seven Dimensions, Five Stages

"The viable system is one that maintains a separate existence in a changing environment."
— Stafford Beer, Brain of the Firm

The framework this book is about has a name. The Integrated Risk and AI Governance Maturity Model. The name is more bureaucratic than the framework. The framework itself is a structured instrument for diagnosing how an enterprise actually governs the AI it is deploying and the risks it is, in fact, exposed to.

It has seven dimensions. It has five maturity stages. It has a small set of rules that hold the dimensions together and prevent the kind of summary score that flatters its subjects. And it has a signature element, deployed identically across all seven dimensions, that surfaces the form-substance gap that ordinary governance assessments leave undisclosed.

This chapter introduces these components at the level required to read the rest of the book. The chapters that follow walk each dimension in turn. Part Three describes the diagnostic patterns that emerge across the dimensions. Part Four describes the work the patterns warrant. For now, the goal is to introduce the framework's structural logic in a way that prepares the reader for the depth that follows.

Figure 1. The framework's structural logic. Six operating dimensions arrayed around the keystone, with each scored on a five- stage maturity scale.

THE SEVEN DIMENSIONS

The framework has seven dimensions. The number is not arbitrary. Each captures a distinct aspect of governance that, in my experience, cannot be reduced to the others without losing diagnostic resolution. Other practitioners may parse the territory differently. They will find their boundaries crossing mine in different places. The seven I have settled on are the ones that, applied seriously, produce findings that other partitions would have missed.

The dimensions are:

POLICY AND ENFORCEMENT

Whether policies exist, whether they are current and accessible, and most importantly whether they actually bind the behavior they nominally govern.

RISK IDENTIFICATION AND ASSESSMENT

How the organization identifies risks, scores them, maintains the register, and uses the register in decisions.

CONTROLS, EVIDENCE, AND CONTINUOUS MONITORING

The design, operation, and monitoring of the controls catalog, including whether the controls demonstrably reduce risk rather than merely operating on schedule.

THIRD-PARTY AND EMBEDDED AI RISK

Vendor risk, with particular attention to the AI-specific extensions that conventional vendor risk programs have not yet absorbed.

AI USE AND LIFECYCLE GOVERNANCE

How AI capabilities are inventoried, classified, approved, monitored, and decommissioned across their lifecycle.

INCIDENT AND ISSUE MANAGEMENT

How the organization responds to incidents and, more consequentially, how it learns from them in ways that produce structural change.

DECISION RIGHTS AND ACCOUNTABILITY

How authority is documented and operationally exercised across the organization, including for the new categories of AI decisions that conventional decision rights frameworks have not absorbed.

I will say more about the last of these. Decision Rights is the keystone. The framework's logic treats it as the dimension on which all the others depend. The argument for that position is the substance of Chapter 11. For now, it is enough to note that the dimension is structurally privileged in the framework and that its position is the result of analytical conviction, not arbitrary ordering.

THE FIVE STAGES

Each dimension is scored on a five-stage maturity scale. The scale is structurally similar to the Capability Maturity Model that Watts Humphrey introduced for software process improvement in the late 1980s. The structural similarity is deliberate. The CMMI tradition has produced the most durable maturity- modeling discipline in the management literature, and there is no reason to start over from scratch.

STAGE 1: REACTIVE

The dimension is not operating in any organized way. Activities occur in response to incidents or external prompting. There is no defined methodology, no consistent operation, no organizational learning.

STAGE 2: DEFINED

The dimension has a defined methodology, documented at the level required to be communicated and followed. The methodology may or may not be operating consistently. The documentation exists.

STAGE 3: MANAGED

The dimension is operating consistently according to the defined methodology. Activities occur on schedule. Evidence is produced. Reports are generated. The methodology is followed.

STAGE 4: INTEGRATED

The dimension is operating consistently and is integrated with adjacent dimensions. Information flows between dimensions. Decisions in one dimension reference inputs from others. The dimensions operate as a system rather than as independent functions.

STAGE 5: ADAPTIVE

The dimension is operating consistently, integrated with adjacent dimensions, and improving over time based on evidence from its own operation. The dimension learns. Structural change is driven by what the dimension itself discovers.

Enterprises typically score in the range of Stage 2 to Stage 3 on most dimensions. Stage 4 is uncommon. Stage 5 is rare. The framework's purpose is not to produce uniformly high scores. It is to identify, with diagnostic specificity, where the organization stands and what the next stage requires.

Stage 3 is good. Stage 4 is excellent. Stage 5 is, in 2026, exceptional.

THE FLOOR RULE AND THE GAP RULE

The framework has two rules that prevent summary scores from flattering their subjects. The rules are simple, applied consistently across dimensions, and produce findings that would otherwise be hidden by averaging.

The floor rule applies within a dimension. It treats the dimension as a system rather than a portfolio: a dimension's effective maturity is constrained by its weakest constituent component, not described by the average across components. Averaging permits a strong component to compensate for a weak one in the score, when the operational reality is the opposite — the weak component limits what the rest of the system can achieve. The floor rule's effect is to prevent the kind of summary score that flatters its subjects by burying their deficits in the arithmetic.

The gap rule applies across a dimension. When the spread between the most mature and least mature components within a dimension is substantial, the unevenness is itself a finding, separate from the dimension's score. A wide spread indicates the dimension is being operated unevenly, with some components developed and others neglected. The neglect usually has structural consequences that the score alone would obscure: it reveals where attention has been concentrated and where it has not, and the asymmetry typically corresponds to where the dimension's failures are concentrated.

The floor rule prevents averaging from hiding deficits. The gap rule surfaces unevenness that the floor rule alone would not capture. Together, the two principles produce a dimension-level picture that reflects how the governance actually operates rather than how the documentation describes it.

THE SIGNATURE ELEMENT

Each dimension has a fifth section, Section E, that is structurally consistent across dimensions and that I have come to call the signature element. Where Sections A through D measure structure and operation, Section E interrogates effectiveness along axes that are calibrated to each dimension but architected to the same logic. Asked seriously and answered honestly, the signature element surfaces the form- substance gap that conventional assessments miss.

The signature element interrogates four families of program behavior that conventional assessments leave unexamined: whether the program learns from its own operation, whether it carries internal dysfunction the team can name but cannot change, whether it can articulate the value of its own contribution with operational specificity, and whether the senior executives nominally responsible for the function are aligned on what the function is for. Each family of question is designed to surface a corresponding failure mode that the form-substance gap conceals.

In Chapter 12, I describe the signature element in greater depth. It is, in my view, the part of the framework that does diagnostic work no other governance maturity framework I know of does. It produces the patterns that Part Three is about. For now, it is enough to know that every dimension has it, in the same position, interrogating the same diagnostic axes in dimension-specific form.

HOW THE FRAMEWORK IS APPLIED

The framework is applied through an assessment engagement. The engagement runs for approximately six weeks. It includes interviews with the program team for each dimension, interviews with the named senior executives, review of documentary evidence, and triangulation across the three sources. The triangulation is essential. Interviews alone produce optimistic findings. Documents alone produce optimistic findings. The combination of interviews with documents and with separate interviews of executives produces findings that hold up under scrutiny.

The engagement produces a current-state maturity profile across the seven dimensions, the cumulative patterns identified across the dimensions, and a prioritized roadmap for remediation. The roadmap is, in practice, the most valuable deliverable. It tells the executive team where to invest first, where to defer, and what to expect from each phase of work.

The engagement does not produce a passing grade. There is no passing grade. There are findings of various kinds, calibrated to the organization's current state. The framework's purpose is not to produce a label. It is to identify the next stage's work and to enable the organization to undertake it deliberately.

◆ ◆ ◆

The chapters that follow walk each dimension in turn. Chapter 5 starts with Policy and Enforcement, the dimension where most enterprises have the most artifacts and the smallest behavioral effect. The pattern is illustrative of what the framework is designed to surface across all seven dimensions.

CHAPTER IN BRIEF

- The framework has seven dimensions and five maturity stages. The structural logic places Decision Rights at the center as the keystone; the other six are operating dimensions that depend on it.
- Two rules prevent summary scores from flattering their subjects. The floor rule treats a dimension as a system whose effective maturity is constrained by its weakest component. The gap rule treats uneven maturity within a dimension as a finding in its own right.
- Every dimension has a signature element in Section E that interrogates effectiveness rather than structure or operation. The signature element is what produces the diagnostic findings the framework is built to generate, and what distinguishes it from conventional maturity models that measure form alone.
- The framework is applied through a six-week engagement combining program-team interviews, executive interviews, and documentary triangulation. The output is a current-state profile and a prioritized roadmap.

CHAPTER V

Policy and Enforcement

"There is the way the world is, the way we say the world is, and the way the world ought to be. Governance lives in the difference between the first two."

— paraphrasing Chris Argyris

Of the seven dimensions, this one is where enterprises have built the most artifacts and produced the smallest behavioral effect. The policy libraries are enormous. The acknowledgment tracking is precise. The communication discipline is well-developed. None of this guarantees that the policies bind the behavior they nominally govern. At many firms, the binding has, over time, become attenuated to the point of invisibility.

This chapter is about the dimension that addresses policy. It explains what the dimension measures, what mature practice looks like, and what the most common findings are. Section E, the signature element, is treated in detail because the form-substance gap is more visible here than in almost any other dimension.

WHY POLICY MATTERS

Policy is the documented expression of what the organization expects of itself. The expectation may concern conduct, process, decision-making, risk acceptance, technology use, or any number of other domains. The policy itself is rarely the operative thing. The operative thing is the behavior the policy is intended to produce. A policy that produces no change in behavior is, functionally, decoration.

Policies are not, however, the same thing as governance. A policy is an explicit statement of what the organization expects. Governance is the system by which the expectation actually shapes behavior. Enterprises have substantial libraries of policies. Many have weak systems for making the policies bind behavior. The gap between the library and the binding is the central concern of this dimension, and it is, in my experience, the gap most CIOs and CROs understate when they think about their own governance posture.

The argument that follows is not that policies are unimportant. The argument is that policies are necessary but not sufficient. Sufficient governance includes the operational mechanisms that translate policy into behavior. The framework measures both. Enterprises score well on the policy side and weakly on the operational side. The unevenness is the typical finding.

WHAT THE DIMENSION MEASURES

The Policy and Enforcement dimension is structured into five sections.

Section A measures the policy library. Coverage across regulatory, operational, and strategic domains. Currency against published revision cycles. Accessibility to the populations the policies bind. Specificity at the level required to guide behavior in the operational contexts where the policies apply.

Section B measures policy development and maintenance. The methodology by which policies are developed. The stakeholders involved. The approval pathways and authority levels. The revision cadence. The versioning discipline.

Section C measures communication and acknowledgment. Whether policies are communicated to the populations they bind. Whether acknowledgment is tracked. Whether training is provided where the policy's substance requires it. Whether refresh communication occurs when policies are revised.

Section D measures enforcement and exception. Whether policy adherence is monitored. Whether non- adherence is detected. Whether exception management operates with appropriate authority by exception type. Whether consequences are applied when material non-adherence occurs.

Section E is the effectiveness section. Whether a policy revision in the past twelve months was driven specifically by evidence from the program rather than by an external requirement. Whether the program team privately believes a current policy is ineffective and cannot, for political reasons, change it. Whether the program can predict, with operational specificity, what would happen if the policy program were eliminated. Whether the executives nominally associated with policy (typically CEO, General Counsel, Chief Compliance Officer) produce aligned answers when asked separately about policy priorities.

WHAT MATURE PRACTICE LOOKS LIKE

Stage 3 in this dimension looks like a thorough policy library, current against documented revision cycles, accessible to bound populations, with documented development methodology and communicated acknowledgment tracking. The dimension is operating. Activities occur on schedule. Evidence is produced. Large enterprises typically operate at Stage 3 on the first four sections.

Stage 4 looks like Stage 3 with integration to adjacent dimensions. The risk register informs policy priorities. The incident program produces policy revision triggers. The audit findings flow into policy updates. The decision rights matrix is consistent with the policy library. The dimensions operate as a system. Stage 4 is uncommon in this dimension because policy programs typically operate in functional isolation from the dimensions that should be informing them.

Stage 5 looks like Stage 4 with structural learning. The policy library is reviewed against operational evidence and revised based on what is found. Policies that are routinely bypassed are surfaced and either enforced or retired. Policies that produce no observable behavioral effect are revised in their language or replaced with alternative mechanisms. The policy program is learning from its own operation.

Stage 5 in this dimension is rare. The structural learning it requires is uncommon. The reasons are political rather than methodological, and they are addressed in the next section.

WHAT THE MOST COMMON FINDINGS ARE

Across the firms in which this framework has been applied, several findings recur with sufficient frequency to be considered modal patterns.

THE COVERAGE-WITHOUT-BINDING PATTERN

The first common finding is that the policy library has excellent coverage and weak binding. The library has policies addressing every domain the organization operates in. The policies are current. They are accessible. The acknowledgment is tracked. And the populations bound by the policies operate, in practice, with substantial deviation from what the policies require. The deviation is not generally hidden. It is visible to anyone who looks. It is, more often than not, not looked at.

The remediation is not to add more policies. The library is already thorough. The remediation is to address the binding mechanism. The mechanism includes monitoring of adherence, detection of deviation, escalation of material deviation, and consequence application. Enterprises have one or two of these components operating and the others either absent or weak. The strengthening of the missing components, more than the further extension of the library, is what produces governance that operates rather than that exists.

THE ACKNOWLEDGMENT-WITHOUT-UNDERSTANDING PATTERN

The second common finding is that acknowledgment tracking is precise and understanding is shallow. The bound population has clicked through the acknowledgment. The training, if any, has been completed. The certification is on file. The substance of the policy is not, in many cases, present in the bound population's working knowledge. The acknowledgment certifies that the person was shown the policy. It does not certify that the person understood the policy or could apply it in the operational contexts where the policy is relevant.

The remediation is to extend the acknowledgment discipline into understanding verification. The verification is more substantial than the acknowledgment. It includes the operational testing of the policy's understanding through scenario-based examples, the targeted training for populations whose understanding is weak, and the iterative improvement of the policy's communication based on the testing results. Few enterprises have made this extension.

THE EXCEPTION-WITHOUT-DISCIPLINE PATTERN

The third common finding is that exception management has been delegated downward without the discipline to support the delegation. The policy specifies that exceptions can be granted at certain authority levels. The granting authority is exercised, in practice, at lower levels than the policy specifies. The pattern is justified, locally, by operational pressure: the higher-level authority is too slow, too busy, too uninterested. The pattern is also, cumulatively, the abandonment of the policy.

The remediation is to bring the exception management back to the specified authority levels and to invest in the operational mechanisms (delegation discipline, decision queues, exception templates) that allow the specified authority to operate at the speed the operations require. The remediation is uncomfortable because it requires the executives who have benefited from informal delegation to take back the authority and exercise it. Few firms have done this. The result is the gradual degradation of the policy's authority over time.

HOW THE DIMENSION INTERACTS WITH THE OTHERS

Policy and Enforcement interacts with several other dimensions. The most consequential interactions are with Decision Rights (which determines who has authority to enforce or grant exceptions), with Risk Identification (which should inform policy priorities), and with Incident Management (which should drive policy revision when patterns of incident reveal policy weaknesses).

When these interactions are weak, the policy program operates in isolation. The policies do not reflect the current risk picture. The exceptions are granted by people whose authority is not what the policy specifies. The incidents do not produce policy revisions. The program continues to operate. Its contribution to governance is, however, limited by the absence of the cross-dimensional flow.

When these interactions are strong, the policy program is one component of a coordinated governance system. The policies reflect the current risk picture. The exceptions are granted with appropriate authority. The incidents drive structural revision. The policies are alive rather than archival.

SECTION E IN DETAIL

The effectiveness section deserves additional treatment because the form-substance gap is most visible here.

On evidence-driven policy revision in the past twelve months, the dimension typically produces a long pause from the program team. The team can identify policy revisions. The revisions were typically triggered by regulatory change, audit finding, or executive directive rather than by evidence from the policy program's own operation. The distinction matters. Revisions driven by external prompting indicate that the policy program is responsive. Revisions driven by internal evidence indicate that the policy program is learning. Enterprises typically operate responsively. Few operate as learning programs.

On the privately-acknowledged ineffective policy, the dimension produces candid responses when asked seriously. Almost every policy program team can identify policies they privately believe to be ineffective. The policies persist for organizational reasons. The senior executive who originally sponsored the policy is still in place. The regulator who expects the policy is still expecting it. The institutional memory of why the policy was created has been lost, and the program team cannot get authorization to retire it. The candid acknowledgment is itself diagnostic. It indicates that the program team has accurate diagnostic capability and limited authority to act on it. This combination, persistent across dimensions, produces the Locked-In pattern that Chapter 13 describes.

On predictive specificity, the dimension produces generic responses. The program asserts that without policies, behavior would deteriorate. The assertion is unobjectionable and unspecific. A program that can articulate, with operational specificity, what behaviors would change and what consequences would follow has done analytical work that few programs have done. The absence of the specificity is not a failure of the program; it is the absence of the analytical work that would make the specificity available. The Unmodeled pattern, also described in Chapter 13, is what often surfaces here.

On executive alignment, the dimension cannot be assessed from the program team's account alone. The finding is produced by interviewing the executives separately and comparing their answers. The interview discipline is part of the engagement methodology. The results are sometimes startling. CEOs and General Counsels operating in the same organization can have substantially different views of what the policy program is for and what it should produce. The misalignment surfaces in the assessment in a way it does not surface in normal executive discourse, because the executives have not previously been asked in the form the assessment requires.

◆◆◆

This dimension produces, in practice, a Stage 2 to Stage 3 score with Section E producing the kind of findings the signature element is designed to produce. The pattern repeats across the dimensions that follow, though the specific findings vary. The next chapter takes up Risk Identification and Assessment, where the pattern produces different specifics but the same shape.

CHAPTER IN BRIEF

- Policy is the documented expression of what an organization expects of itself. Governance is the system that makes the expectation actually shape behavior. The gap between the library and the binding is this dimension's central concern.
- The three modal patterns are: coverage without binding (the library is thorough but behavior deviates), acknowledgment without understanding (the population has clicked through but cannot apply the policy), and exception without discipline (exceptions are granted at lower authority than the policy specifies).
- Stage 5 in this dimension is rare. It requires the structural learning that retires policies that no longer bind behavior — which is political work, not methodological work.
- Section E in this dimension reliably surfaces both the Locked-In pattern (the team knows the dysfunction but cannot address it) and the Unmodeled pattern (the program cannot predict what would happen without it).

CHAPTER VI

Risk Identification and Assessment

"What we don't know we don't know is generally more dangerous than what we know we don't know."
— Nassim Nicholas Taleb

The risk register is the artifact every CRO can produce. The register is current. It is structured. It is reviewed periodically. It informs reports to the board, the audit committee, the executive committee. The register is the most visible product of the risk management function and the artifact most likely to be cited as evidence that risk is being managed.

The register is not, at most firms, a particularly accurate description of the risks the organization is actually exposed to. It is a useful approximation, at some firms. At others, it is an artifact that lives parallel to the actual risk picture without substantially affecting decisions. This dimension assesses the difference.

The dimension is structured the same way as Policy and Enforcement. Five sections. A first four that address structure and operation, a fifth that addresses effectiveness. The findings, again, tend to cluster at Stage 2 to Stage 3 with the effectiveness section producing the deepest insights.

WHAT RISK IDENTIFICATION IS SUPPOSED TO DO

Risk identification, properly conducted, is the systematic effort to know what the organization is exposed to. The effort begins with the categories of risk the organization faces (financial, operational, strategic, regulatory, reputational, technological, and others). It proceeds through the specific risks within each category (concentrated counterparty exposure within financial; key-person dependency within operational; market-shift exposure within strategic; and so on).

The effort is not, at most firms, conducted in this systematic way. The risk register is, more often than not, the cumulative residue of past risk events, audit findings, regulatory directives, and individual contributions from the risk team's professional judgment. The categorization is partial. The within-category enumeration is incomplete. The register reflects what has come to attention rather than what is actually exposed.

This is not, by itself, a failure. The risk function operates within finite attention. The register is the artifact of where that attention has been focused. The failure, when it occurs, is the failure to recognize that the register is a partial artifact and to construct the methodology that would extend it toward completeness.

WHAT THE DIMENSION MEASURES

Section A measures the identification methodology. Cadence of identification activities. Inputs to identification including incident learning, audit findings, environmental scanning, and front-line input. Coverage across enterprise, business unit, and operational levels. The substance of identification rather than its appearance.

Section B measures assessment and scoring. The methodology by which identified risks are scored. The calibration of likelihood and impact dimensions. The aggregation methodology. The currency of assessments against documented update cadence.

Section C measures the register and reporting. The register's completeness against the identification methodology. The reporting from the register to executive and board audiences. The visualization and prioritization in reporting.

Section D measures decision integration. Whether risk information is actually used in consequential decisions. Whether documented references to the register appear in decision records. Whether risk appetite is operationalized at the points of decision.

Section E is the effectiveness section. Evidence-driven revision of the identification methodology. Privately-acknowledged risks that the program cannot, for political reasons, escalate. Predictive specificity of the program's elimination consequences. Executive alignment on top risks across CEO, CRO, CFO, and the board.

WHAT MATURE PRACTICE LOOKS LIKE

Stage 3 in this dimension looks like a structured identification methodology operating on a defined cadence, with a scored register, regular reporting, and some integration with consequential decisions. Large enterprises typically operate at Stage 3 on the first three sections of the dimension. Section D, decision integration, is where Stage 3 organizations are typically weakest.

Stage 4 requires the integration of the risk function with the consequential decision flow of the organization. The risk register is not, at Stage 4, an artifact that is reported on. It is an instrument that informs decisions. Senior decision-makers reference the register in their decisions. Risk appetite, expressed in operational limits, is visible at the points of decision. Risk findings drive structural change in controls, vendors, and other adjacent dimensions.

Stage 5 requires the methodology to learn from its own operation. Risks that materialize but were not in the register lead to methodology revisions. Risks in the register that do not materialize, over reasonable time periods, lead to register revisions. The methodology is examined for its predictive validity and adjusted when the validity is found wanting. This is rare. Few enterprises have constructed the analytical capability to undertake this kind of methodology examination.

THE MOST COMMON FINDINGS

THE REGISTER-WITHOUT-DECISION PATTERN

The most common finding is that the register is maintained and the decisions are not informed by it. The risk team produces the register. The register is reviewed. The reports are circulated. The senior decision- makers, when making consequential decisions, do not consult the register. They make decisions based on the business case, the operational considerations, the political dynamics, and their own judgment about what the risks are. The register is, in effect, parallel to the decision flow.

The remediation is to make the register operationally relevant at the points of decision. The relevance requires the register to be visible in the decision workflow, the relevant risks to be retrievable in real time, and the risk appetite to be operationalized in a form that constrains decisions rather than just describes them. The remediation is substantially a workflow and instrumentation problem rather than a risk-methodology problem. Few firms have undertaken the workflow work.

THE METHODOLOGY-WITHOUT-CALIBRATION PATTERN

The second common finding is that the scoring methodology has not been calibrated against materialized risks. The methodology assigns likelihood and impact scores using a scale that has not been validated against historical materializations. The methodology may, in fact, be systematically over- or under-estimating either dimension. The risk team is not analytically positioned to know.

The remediation is the calibration work. The historical materializations are reviewed. The pre- materialization scores are retrieved. The actual outcomes are compared. The methodology is adjusted where the comparison reveals systematic bias. The work is straightforward and rare. Few risk functions have undertaken it.

THE AGGREGATION-WITHOUT-INSIGHT PATTERN

The third common finding is that the register's aggregation produces summary statistics that obscure the patterns that matter most. The top ten risks are reported. The aggregate exposure is summed. The trend is plotted. None of these aggregations, at many firms, surfaces the concentration patterns that produce the most consequential losses (multiple risks materializing simultaneously, correlated risks producing cascading consequences, second-order risks from primary materializations).

The remediation is the construction of aggregation techniques that surface the patterns that matter. Stress testing. Scenario analysis. Concentration analysis across risk categories. Correlation analysis. The techniques are well-developed in financial services and less so in other industries. The Phase Two work I describe in Chapter 17 includes the construction of these techniques in dimensions where they have not previously been applied.

HOW THE DIMENSION INTERACTS WITH THE OTHERS

Risk Identification interacts strongly with Incident Management (incidents are evidence about risk), with Controls (controls address identified risks), with Decision Rights (risk acceptance requires defined authority), and with Policy (policies address risks in defined ways).

When these interactions are weak, the risk function operates in functional isolation. The register is maintained without inputs from incidents. The controls catalog is maintained without reference to the register. The decision authority for risk acceptance is documented in the policy library without operational mechanisms. The function continues to operate. The contribution to governance is limited by the absence of the cross-dimensional flow.

When these interactions are strong, the risk function is the analytical center of the governance program. The register reflects the cumulative input from incidents, audits, environmental scanning, and front-line judgment. The controls catalog addresses the registered risks. The decision authority operates against the registered risks at the appropriate thresholds. The policies bind behavior in ways that the register identifies as warranted. The function is connected. The connection is what produces governance.

SECTION E IN DETAIL

On evidence-driven methodology revision, the dimension produces examples that don't quite fit. The team identifies revisions; the revisions are driven by changes in the business, by regulatory updates, by external consulting recommendations. The category of revision in scope — revision driven by the methodology's own performance against its predictions — is uncommon. The methodology is operating. The methodology is not learning.

On the privately-acknowledged unaddressable risk, the dimension produces candid responses when asked under conditions of confidentiality. The risk team is, more often than not, aware of risks that have not been escalated for political reasons. The risks may involve executives whose attention would be unwelcome. They may involve business areas whose performance depends on the risk's continued non- escalation. They may involve regulatory areas where the organization's exposure is genuinely problematic and where the escalation would force a conversation the organization is not yet ready to have.

On predictive specificity of program elimination consequences, the dimension produces generic responses in most cases. The risk function asserts that, without it, risks would materialize. The assertion is unobjectionable and unspecific. The specific risks that would materialize, the specific decisions that would be made worse, the specific exposures that would increase — these articulations require analytical work the risk function has not generally done.

On executive alignment, the dimension produces particularly consequential findings. The CEO, the CRO, the CFO, and the board chair operating in the same organization can have substantially different views of what the top risks are. The differences are not generally surfaced in normal executive discourse because the topic of risk is treated abstractly. The assessment, conducted with separate interviews, surfaces the differences. The differences are typically large enough to matter and have rarely been previously addressed.

Risk Identification is, in my experience, the dimension where the form-substance gap is most consequential, because the consequences of the gap include risks that materialize and damage the organization. The remediation requires the integration of the dimension with the others and the construction of analytical capability that, at many firms, is missing. The next chapter takes up Controls, Evidence, and Continuous Monitoring — the dimension where the form-substance gap is most easily measured and, surprisingly often, not measured at all.

CHAPTER IN BRIEF

- Risk identification is the systematic effort to know what the organization is exposed to. At most firms, the register is the residue of what has come to attention rather than the output of systematic enumeration.
- The three modal patterns are: register without decision (the register exists parallel to actual decisions), methodology without calibration (the scoring has not been validated against materialized risks), and aggregation without insight (the summaries hide the concentration patterns that matter).
- Stage 4 in this dimension requires the register to inform consequential decisions in real time. Few firms have done the workflow and instrumentation work that would make this possible.
- Section E's interrogation of executive alignment produces particularly consequential findings here. CEOs, CROs, CFOs, and board chairs at the same firm routinely hold substantially different views of the top risks — views that rarely surface in normal discourse.

CHAPTER VII

Controls, Evidence, and Continuous Monitoring

"We measure what we can, and we manage what we measure. The trouble is, in governance, those are rarely the same things."
— Robert Kaplan

Of all seven dimensions, this one has been most shaped by external regulatory pressure. Sarbanes-Oxley in the early 2000s, and the parallel regulations in other jurisdictions, forced public companies to develop the discipline of designing, operating, documenting, and evidencing controls over financial reporting. Two decades later, the discipline has matured into a recognizable corporate function. Internal audit. SOX testing. Control documentation. Evidence collection. The function operates with substantial professionalization at most large enterprises.

The maturity of the function is genuine. The function's contribution to risk reduction is, at many firms, less clear than the maturity of the function would suggest. The controls catalog has grown over time. The growth has been additive rather than discriminating. Controls have been added in response to incidents, audit findings, and regulatory updates. Controls have rarely been retired. The catalog is, at most enterprises, larger than the risk picture warrants, with substantial overlap, redundancy, and controls whose contribution to risk reduction cannot be demonstrated.

This chapter is about the dimension that addresses this. It explains what the dimension measures, what mature practice looks like, and what the most common findings are. The signature element in this dimension produces some of the most diagnostically powerful findings the framework generates, because the willingness to retire controls is the central test the dimension applies.

WHAT THE DIMENSION MEASURES

Section A measures the catalog. Completeness across risk-bearing processes. Organization and accessibility. Ownership and maintenance discipline.

Section B measures design. Whether controls are designed with explicit specification of the risk they address, the mechanism by which they reduce the risk, and the evidence they will produce. Whether effectiveness criteria are part of the design rather than added afterward.

Section C measures operation. Whether controls operate against their documented cadence. Whether evidence is collected. Whether evidence is retained and accessible.

Section D measures continuous monitoring. Whether monitoring infrastructure exists across the catalog. Whether alerting operates on control deviation. Whether pattern analysis is conducted across the monitoring outputs.

Section E is the effectiveness section. Whether a control has been retired in the past twelve months specifically for proven ineffectiveness. Whether a structured exercise has surfaced controls the program privately believes are ineffective. Whether the three most expensive controls in the catalog have demonstrable evidence of risk reduction. Whether the organization can predict which risks would materialize first if the control program were eliminated. Whether the named executives in this dimension (chief audit executive, CISO, CIO) are aligned on the five most critical controls.

WHAT MATURE PRACTICE LOOKS LIKE

Stage 3 in this dimension is common in audit-mature organizations. The catalog is current. The controls operate on schedule. The evidence is collected. The annual SOX cycle is completed. The dimension is, by these measures, operating.

Stage 4 requires the catalog to be measurably contributing to risk reduction. Not just operating. Producing demonstrable risk reduction outcomes. The integration is with the risk register (the controls address registered risks), with the incident program (control failures trigger control redesign), with the policy library (policies and controls are consistent), and with the decision rights matrix (control exception authority is operationally exercised).

Stage 5 requires the catalog to be learning. Controls that produce no demonstrable risk reduction are retired. Controls that produce evidence of failure are redesigned. New controls are designed against effectiveness criteria. The catalog, over time, becomes smaller and more potent rather than larger and more diffuse.

The willingness to retire controls is the central test that distinguishes the Stage 5 organizations.

Stage 5 in this dimension is rare. The kind of catalog management it requires is uncommon. Few firms have catalogs that have grown over time and have, in practice, ever retired controls. The willingness to retire is itself the test that distinguishes the Stage 5 organizations.

THE MOST COMMON FINDINGS

THE CATALOG-INFLATION PATTERN

The first common finding is that the catalog has inflated over time without corresponding deflation. Controls have been added. Controls have rarely been retired. The cumulative catalog includes overlapping controls (multiple controls addressing the same risk), redundant controls (the same control documented in multiple places), and obsolete controls (controls addressing risks that no longer exist or that have been mitigated by structural change).

The remediation is the catalog review work I describe in Chapter 17. The review examines each control against its risk reduction evidence. Controls without evidence are flagged for redesign or retirement. Controls with evidence are confirmed. The catalog, after the review, is smaller and more potent than the catalog that entered the review. The reduction is itself diagnostic. It indicates that the program has the analytical capability and the political authority to retire controls.

THE OPERATION-WITHOUT-EFFECTIVENESS PATTERN

The second common finding is that controls operate without demonstrable effectiveness. The controls run on schedule. The evidence is collected. The audit confirms that the controls are designed and operating. What the audit does not confirm — because the audit methodology is not built for it — is whether the controls are reducing the risks they nominally address. The operation is confirmed. The effectiveness is assumed.

The remediation is the effectiveness measurement work. Effectiveness is measured against the risk the control addresses. The measurement requires the construction of evidence that the risk is, in fact, being reduced by the control's operation. The measurement is, at many firms, a new capability. The construction of the capability is part of the Phase Two work.

THE CONTINUOUS-MONITORING-WITHOUT-CONTINUITY PATTERN

The third common finding is that the continuous monitoring infrastructure has been built but is not, in practice, monitoring continuously. The infrastructure was implemented. The alerting was configured. The dashboards were built. The actual continuous monitoring — the daily attention to the monitoring output, the response to alerts, the pattern analysis across outputs — has been intermittent. The infrastructure exists. The monitoring discipline does not.

The remediation is the construction of the monitoring discipline. The discipline includes the staffing of the monitoring function with people whose primary task is to attend to the output, the construction of the response playbooks for the alerts the monitoring produces, and the integration of the monitoring with the incident response capability. The discipline is operationally substantial and is, at many firms, the missing component.

HOW THE DIMENSION INTERACTS WITH THE OTHERS

Controls interact with Risk Identification (controls address risks), with Incident Management (control failures produce incidents and incidents reveal control gaps), with Policy (controls implement policies), and with Decision Rights (control exceptions require defined authority).

The interaction with Incident Management is the most consequential and the most commonly weak. Incidents are, in principle, the evidence about which controls are working and which are not. The pattern of incidents over time should drive control redesign. At many firms, control redesign is driven by audit findings rather than by incident patterns. The audit findings address compliance with documented controls. The incidents reveal which controls are operationally effective. The two are not equivalent. The use of audit findings as the primary input to redesign produces a catalog that is audit-defensible and operationally weak. The use of incident patterns as the primary input would produce a catalog that is operationally strong and audit-defensible. Most firms have made the first choice. The second is the work the framework recommends.

SECTION E IN DETAIL

On control retirement in the past twelve months for proven ineffectiveness, the dimension produces no examples. The catalog has grown. Controls have been added. Controls have not been retired. The team can produce examples of controls that were modified or replaced. They cannot, in most cases, produce examples of controls retired specifically because the controls were ineffective. The absence is the finding.

On the privately-acknowledged ineffective controls, the dimension produces lists when asked seriously. The control program team knows, more often than not, which controls in the catalog are operating without demonstrable effectiveness. The controls persist because retiring them would require an audit conversation no one wants to have, or because a senior executive sponsors the control, or because the institutional memory of why the control was created has been lost and no one is willing to be the person who proposes its retirement. The list of these controls is itself diagnostic. Firms whose list is long have the Catalog-Inflation pattern in mature form.

On the demonstrable effectiveness of the three most expensive controls, the dimension produces, in most cases, the discovery that the evidence has not been assembled. The three most expensive controls are typically identifiable from the budget. The evidence that they are reducing the risks they address is typically not assembled. The control owners can produce evidence of operation. They cannot produce evidence of effectiveness. The distinction is the finding.

On executive alignment regarding the five most critical controls, the dimension produces divergent answers. The chief audit executive's list reflects audit attention. The CISO's list reflects security-driven controls. The CIO's list reflects technology operations. The lists overlap in some places and not in others. The non-overlapping items are diagnostic. Each executive considers some controls critical that other executives consider routine. The misalignment is the finding.

◆ ◆ ◆

Controls is the dimension where the form-substance gap is most easily quantified and most rarely quantified. The quantification work is the work the dimension recommends. The next chapter takes up Third-Party and Embedded AI Risk, where the conventional vendor risk discipline is being stressed by the AI-specific extensions that few firms have yet absorbed.

CHAPTER IN BRIEF

- The controls discipline matured under Sarbanes-Oxley and parallel regulations. The function is professional. Its contribution to actual risk reduction is, at most firms, less clear than its operational maturity suggests.
- The three modal patterns are: catalog inflation (additions without retirements), operation without effectiveness (controls run on schedule but their risk reduction is assumed rather than evidenced), and continuous monitoring without continuity (the infrastructure exists but the daily discipline does not).
- The willingness to retire controls is the central test. Firms that have retired controls in the past twelve months for proven ineffectiveness have the analytical capability and political authority that Stage 5 requires. Few firms have.
- The interaction with Incident Management is consequential. Audit findings drive control redesign at most firms; incident patterns rarely do. The shift from audit-driven to incident-driven redesign is the most consequential structural improvement available in this dimension.

CHAPTER VIII

Third-Party and Embedded AI Risk

"We have not eliminated risk by outsourcing it. We have, in many cases, made the risk we now bear less visible to the people responsible for governing it."

— an audit committee chair, in conversation

A surprising amount of enterprise risk now lives outside the enterprise. The risk is borne by the enterprise; the operation is conducted by third parties. The arrangement is, in principle, manageable. The vendor risk management discipline has matured over the past decade and produces, at most large enterprises, a recognizable program with assessment workflows, contractual instruments, and ongoing monitoring.

The discipline has not, in most cases, absorbed the changes that AI has introduced. Conventional vendor risk assumed that vendors provided defined services within defined boundaries. AI vendors provide services whose behavior changes over time, whose capabilities expand without explicit notification, and whose failure modes cascade across customer organizations in ways that conventional vendor failure modes do not.

The conventional vendor risk discipline can be extended for AI. The extension is non-trivial. Most enterprises have not made the extension or have made it partially. The gap between conventional vendor risk and the AI-extended vendor risk is one of the most consequential governance gaps in 2026.

WHAT THE DIMENSION MEASURES

Section A measures the vendor inventory and classification. Whether all vendors are identified, including the fourth-party and beyond relationships. Whether the inventory distinguishes vendors by criticality, AI involvement, and data exposure.

Section B measures the assessment methodology. The pre-engagement due diligence. The contractual instruments. The ongoing assessment cadence. The scoping of assessment to vendor criticality.

Section C measures the AI-specific extensions. The vendor-specific AI inventory (which AI capabilities are provided by each vendor). The contractual provisions addressing AI model behavior, AI training data, AI model updates, and AI failure modes. The assessment of vendor AI governance maturity. The treatment of embedded AI within software licensed for non-AI purposes.

Section D measures incident response and concentration. Vendor-specific incident response playbooks. Vendor concentration analysis. Substitutability planning. Geographic concentration. AI-vendor concentration as a special case.

Section E is the effectiveness section. Termination of a critical vendor in the past twenty-four months for governance reasons. Privately-acknowledged vendor risk concerns the program cannot escalate. Predictive specificity on vendor-failure consequences. Executive alignment across CIO, CRO, General Counsel, and Chief Procurement Officer.

WHY AI CHANGES THE VENDOR RISK PROBLEM

Vendor risk has, until recently, addressed vendors whose services were defined and whose failure modes were bounded. The vendor provided a service, the service was contractually specified, and the failure modes were specific to the contracted service. The risk management was substantially about contractual terms, due diligence on the vendor's operational maturity, and monitoring of service quality.

AI vendors are different in four specific ways. First, their service behavior changes over time without explicit notification. The AI model is retrained or fine-tuned by the vendor, and the customer organization experiences different behavior from the same service. The contractual specification of the service, written at the time of contracting, no longer accurately describes the service being delivered.

Second, the vendor's failure modes cascade across customers. A foundation model vendor whose model produces problematic outputs affects every customer using the model. The failure is not localized to one customer. The remediation by the vendor affects all customers at once. The customer-by-customer impact analysis is harder.

Third, AI capabilities are embedded in software licensed for non-AI purposes. The customer organization has, often unwittingly, accepted AI capabilities as part of a contract that did not foreground them. The Microsoft Copilot deployment that a CRO did not know was AI. The Salesforce Einstein activation that did not trigger AI governance review. The ServiceNow Now Assist enablement that no one mentioned to the audit committee. Each is technically covered by the existing vendor contract. None was, at most firms, subjected to the AI governance discipline.

Fourth, the boundary between the vendor's service and the customer's operations has become porous. AI agents that take actions across customer systems. AI assistants that participate in customer workflows. AI capabilities that connect to customer data in ways that produce hybrid systems where the vendor's contribution and the customer's contribution cannot be cleanly separated. The traditional vendor-customer boundary, which the contract documents, has become operationally fuzzy.

THE MOST COMMON FINDINGS

THE EMBEDDED-AI PATTERN

The most common finding in this dimension is the discovery that the AI inventory — the inventory of AI capabilities deployed in the firm — is substantially smaller than the AI footprint that actually exists. The discrepancy comes from embedded AI. The vendors that the firm contracts with provide software whose AI capabilities are part of the software's standard feature set. The capabilities were activated, in most cases, without explicit decision by the customer organization. They are not on the AI inventory. They are, however, operating.

The Microsoft Copilot example is the most visible because it has been the subject of public discussion. The pattern is identical for Salesforce Einstein, ServiceNow Now Assist, and dozens of other embedded AI capabilities that vendors have introduced over the past two years. The patterns is also identical for a long tail of less-visible embedded AI in HR systems, supply chain platforms, financial planning tools, and customer service applications. The cumulative embedded AI footprint, at large enterprises, is typically two to five times larger than the AI inventory the firm maintains.

The remediation requires a discovery exercise. The exercise is conducted across major vendors, with documented questions about AI capabilities, AI training data use, and AI behavior commitments. The exercise produces a fuller inventory. The fuller inventory is then assessed against the AI governance framework. Many of the embedded capabilities require remediation. Some require contractual adjustment. A few may, on assessment, require activation reversal. The exercise is not a one-time effort. The vendors continue to introduce new AI capabilities. The discovery exercise must recur.

THE CONTRACTUAL-INSUFFICIENCY PATTERN

The second common finding is that contracts with AI vendors do not adequately address AI-specific concerns. The contracts were typically signed before the AI capabilities were activated, or before AI governance attention reached the relevant scope. The contracts include standard provisions for service quality, data protection, and termination. They do not include provisions for AI model behavior, AI training data, model update notification, or AI-specific failure modes. The provisions exist in template language some firms have developed. The provisions have not, in most cases, been incorporated into the existing contracts.

The remediation is a contract renegotiation exercise focused on critical AI vendors. The renegotiation introduces the AI-specific provisions. The provisions are not, in most cases, accepted in full by the vendors. The negotiation produces compromises. The compromises are themselves diagnostic. They indicate where the customer's contractual leverage is sufficient and where it is not. Customers without significant contractual leverage face concentration risk that their procurement function should have surfaced earlier.

THE CONCENTRATION-WITHOUT-SUBSTITUTION PATTERN

The third common finding is that AI vendor concentration has emerged without corresponding substitution planning. The firm is dependent on one foundation model vendor for AI capabilities across multiple business processes. The dependency is sometimes contractual (the vendor's API is integrated into the firm's applications) and sometimes operational (the firm's AI talent is trained on the vendor's tools). The dependency has implications for vendor failure scenarios and for vendor pricing power. The implications have, in most cases, not been substantially analyzed.

The remediation is the substitution planning. The planning produces, for each critical AI capability, an identified alternative provider, an estimated transition cost, an estimated transition time, and an articulated trigger condition for considering the transition. The planning does not, in most cases, lead to actual transition. It produces the analytical posture that makes transition possible if circumstances warrant. The posture itself reduces vendor concentration risk, because the vendor knows the customer has the analytical posture.

SECTION E IN DETAIL

On critical vendor termination in the past twenty-four months, the dimension produces no examples. Vendor termination at the critical level is uncommon. When it occurs, it is typically driven by service quality failures rather than by governance failures. Termination for governance reasons is rare. The absence of examples is diagnostic. It indicates that the vendor risk program does not, in practice, exercise the termination authority that the program nominally has.

On the privately-acknowledged unaddressable vendor concern, the dimension produces candid responses when asked seriously. The vendor risk team is, more often than not, aware of vendor concerns that have not been escalated for political reasons. The vendor may have a senior executive sponsor whose attention to the concern would be unwelcome. The vendor may be embedded in operational dependencies that make termination practically impossible. The vendor may be the subject of an enterprise agreement whose renegotiation would surface broader procurement concerns the organization is not prepared to address.

On predictive specificity regarding vendor failure, the dimension produces more specific responses than do other dimensions. The vendor risk function has typically conducted some scenario analysis on critical vendor failure. The analysis is more developed for some vendors (typically the largest enterprise software vendors) than others. The variance in the specificity is itself diagnostic. It indicates which vendors the function has attended to and which it has not.

On executive alignment across CIO, CRO, General Counsel, and Chief Procurement Officer, the dimension produces particularly consequential findings. The four executives operating in the same organization can have substantially different views of vendor priorities and vendor risks. The Chief Procurement Officer is typically focused on cost and contract terms. The CIO is typically focused on service quality and integration. The CRO is typically focused on operational and concentration risk. The General Counsel is typically focused on contractual and regulatory risk. The four views, brought together, produce a fuller picture than any one view alone. The bringing-together has, in practice, not previously occurred. The misalignment is the finding.

◆ ◆ ◆

Vendor risk for AI is the dimension where the conventional discipline is being most clearly stressed by the technology that has entered the enterprise since the discipline was constructed. The extension required is substantial. The next chapter takes up AI Use and Lifecycle Governance, the dimension that addresses the AI capabilities the firm has consciously deployed (as distinct from the embedded AI this chapter has been substantially about).

CHAPTER IN BRIEF

- Conventional vendor risk management was built for vendors whose services were defined and whose failure modes were bounded. AI vendors are different in four ways: service behavior that changes over time, failure modes that cascade across customers, AI embedded in software licensed for non-AI purposes, and porous boundaries between vendor service and customer operations.
- The three modal patterns are: embedded AI (the AI footprint is two to five times the inventory), contractual insufficiency (existing contracts do not address AI-specific concerns), and concentration without substitution (dependencies have emerged without alternative-provider planning).
- Critical vendor termination for governance reasons is rare. The absence of examples is diagnostic; it indicates the program does not exercise the termination authority it nominally has.
- The bringing-together of CIO, CRO, General Counsel, and Chief Procurement Officer views on vendor priorities is, at most firms, the assessment's most consequential single act in this dimension.

CHAPTER IX

AI Use and Lifecycle Governance

"What gets approved is not always what gets deployed. What gets deployed is not always what stays deployed. Governance is the discipline of keeping the three things in alignment."
— from the methodology

This is the dimension where AI is the explicit subject. The other dimensions address governance functions that AI has stressed without being the primary subject of the function. Here, AI is what the function exists to govern. The dimension is, in most enterprises, the most recently constructed of the seven, and it shows. Many AI governance programs were stood up in 2023 or 2024 in response to public attention on generative AI. Three years is not enough time, at most firms, to reach Stage 3 across all five sections of the dimension.

This chapter describes the dimension's structure, its mature operation, and the modal findings. The dimension addresses the full lifecycle: identification of AI capabilities, classification by risk and use case, approval workflows, ongoing monitoring, model update management, and decommissioning. Each component requires capability that, at most firms, is partial.

WHAT THE DIMENSION MEASURES

Section A measures the AI inventory. Identification methodology, including the discovery of embedded AI. Classification by risk tier and use case category. Currency against ongoing AI activity in the firm. Coverage across the firm's full AI footprint.

Section B measures approval workflows. The criteria by which AI capabilities are approved. The authority that approves. The workflow that routes approval requests. The documentation produced by the approval process.

Section C measures ongoing monitoring. The performance monitoring infrastructure. The behavior monitoring for drift and degradation. The fairness and bias monitoring where applicable. The output review for high-consequence categories.

Section D measures lifecycle management. The model update process. The fine-tuning governance. The decommissioning process. The lifecycle documentation.

Section E is the effectiveness section. AI capability decommissioning in the past twelve months for evidence-based reasons. Privately-acknowledged AI capabilities the program believes should not be running. Predictive specificity on what would happen without the AI governance program. Executive alignment on AI strategy among CEO, CIO, CRO, and Chief Data Officer.

WHAT MATURE PRACTICE LOOKS LIKE

Stage 3 in this dimension means the inventory is current, the approval workflow operates, the monitoring infrastructure is in place, and lifecycle management is documented. At firms that built their AI governance program early (2022 or 2023), Stage 3 is achievable by 2026. At firms that started later, Stage 3 is typically a 2027 target.

Stage 4 requires integration with the rest of the governance system. The AI inventory informs vendor risk decisions. The risk register includes AI-specific risks identified through the inventory. The controls catalog includes AI-specific controls connected to the AI risks. The incident program responds to AI incidents with structural learning. The decision rights matrix covers AI decision categories. Each integration is non-trivial. Stage 4 is uncommon.

Stage 5 requires the AI governance program to learn from its own operation. AI capabilities that produce no demonstrable value are decommissioned. Approval criteria are revised based on what subsequent AI behavior reveals about the original criteria's adequacy. Monitoring infrastructure is improved based on what monitoring outputs surface. The program is, in operation, generating evidence that drives its own structural change. Stage 5 is rare.

THE MOST COMMON FINDINGS

THE INVENTORY-COMPLETENESS PATTERN

The most common finding, observed in practice across many firms, is that the AI inventory is substantially incomplete. The incompleteness is partially structural (embedded AI is not surfaced through the inventory methodology) and partially operational (the inventory methodology depends on team submissions that have not been comprehensive). The cumulative effect is that the inventory captures, at most firms, twenty to fifty percent of the actual AI footprint.

The remediation is the discovery exercise described in the previous chapter, combined with the construction of an inventory methodology that does not rely solely on team submissions. The methodology includes automated discovery of AI activations in software platforms, mandatory disclosure requirements for software acquisitions and renewals, and periodic comprehensive surveys of AI-adjacent function leaders. The combination produces an inventory that approaches completeness rather than the partial inventory that team submissions alone produce.

THE APPROVAL-WITHOUT-CONDITIONS PATTERN

The second common finding is that AI approvals are granted without the conditions that would make subsequent monitoring meaningful. The approval is recorded. The conditions under which the approval was granted are not explicit. When the AI's behavior subsequently changes, the question of whether the new behavior is still within the approved scope cannot be answered, because the approved scope was not, in the original approval, defined with sufficient specificity.

The remediation is the construction of approval criteria that include explicit specifications of behavior boundaries, training data conditions, use case scope, and monitoring requirements. The criteria are then carried forward through the lifecycle. Subsequent behavior is evaluated against the criteria. Behavior outside the criteria triggers re-approval. The discipline is straightforward and rare.

THE MONITORING-WITHOUT-ACTION PATTERN

The third common finding is that AI monitoring infrastructure exists and produces outputs that are not, in practice, acted upon. The dashboards exist. The drift detection runs. The fairness metrics are computed. The outputs accumulate in the monitoring system. The team that should be acting on the outputs has not constructed the response playbooks, the escalation pathways, or the staffing model that would allow the action to occur. The monitoring operates. The acting-on-monitoring does not.

The remediation is the construction of the response capability. Each monitoring output category has a defined response. The response is operationalized in the form of playbooks, decision trees, and staffing. The acting-on-monitoring becomes routine rather than ad hoc. The capability is operationally substantial and, at most firms, is partial.

SECTION E IN DETAIL

On AI capability decommissioning in the past twelve months, the dimension produces no examples. AI capabilities, once deployed, tend to persist. Decommissioning is uncommon. When it occurs, it is typically driven by vendor change rather than by governance evaluation. The absence of decommissioning examples is itself diagnostic. It indicates that the governance program does not, in practice, exercise the decommissioning authority that the program nominally has.

On privately-acknowledged AI capabilities that should not be running, the dimension produces lists when asked under conditions of candor. The AI governance program team is, more often than not, aware of AI capabilities that are operating without producing the value the original deployment promised, with monitoring that has revealed problematic behavior, or with use cases that have expanded beyond the originally approved scope. The capabilities persist because their decommissioning would surface the original approval as having been mistaken, or because a senior executive sponsors the capability, or because the operational dependencies that have built up around the capability make its removal practically difficult.

On predictive specificity regarding AI governance elimination, the dimension produces generic responses in most cases. The AI governance program asserts that, without it, AI risks would materialize. The specific risks, the specific decisions that would be made worse, the specific consequences — these articulations have not been undertaken. The absence is part of the Unmodeled pattern described in Chapter 13.

On executive alignment among CEO, CIO, CRO, and Chief Data Officer, the dimension produces particularly divergent answers. The four executives operating in the same organization can have substantially different views of what AI is for in the firm, what risks it presents, and what governance is supposed to produce. The CEO's view is typically strategic and acceleration-oriented. The CIO's view is typically execution-oriented and capability-focused. The CRO's view is typically risk-mitigation-focused. The Chief Data Officer's view is typically data-quality and analytical-capability focused. The four views, brought together, can produce productive tension. They more often, in practice, produce ongoing misalignment that limits the AI program's effectiveness.

◆◆◆

AI Use and Lifecycle Governance is the dimension where the firm's relationship with AI is most directly tested. The findings are typically more uncomfortable than the findings in other dimensions, because the dimension is what the AI governance committee was nominally constructed to address. The next chapter takes up Incident and Issue Management — the dimension that produces the evidence about what has gone wrong and that drives, when it operates well, the structural learning that the framework's Stage 5 requires.

CHAPTER IN BRIEF

- The AI Use dimension is the most recently constructed of the seven at most enterprises. Three years is rarely enough time to reach Stage 3 across all five sections.
- The three modal patterns are: inventory incompleteness (the captured inventory is twenty to fifty percent of the actual footprint), approval without conditions (the approved scope was not defined with enough specificity to enable later monitoring), and monitoring without action (the dashboards exist but the response capability does not).
- AI capability decommissioning in the past twelve months is uncommon. The absence is diagnostic: the governance program does not exercise the decommissioning authority it nominally has.
- Executive misalignment is particularly consequential in this dimension. The four named executives — CEO, CIO, CRO, Chief Data Officer — routinely hold substantially different views of what AI is for, what risks it presents, and what governance should produce.

CHAPTER X

Incident and Issue Management

"Every system is perfectly designed to get the results it gets. The incidents are the system telling you what it's designed for."
— W. Edwards Deming, paraphrased

Incidents are the empirical evidence about governance. They are what the organization actually experiences when its risk management, controls, and policies meet operational reality. Incidents that occur reveal the gaps in the system that produced them. Incidents that recur reveal the failure of the system to learn from prior occurrences.

This is, in my view, the most under-leveraged dimension in the framework. Incidents contain extraordinary information about how the organization is governed. The information is, in most cases, not extracted. The incident is responded to, closed, and filed. The structural learning that should follow does not, in many cases, occur. The same kinds of incidents recur. The same root causes are documented again. The cumulative organizational learning is far smaller than the cumulative incident experience would support.

WHAT THE DIMENSION MEASURES

Section A measures detection. Whether incidents are detected when they occur. Whether the detection covers the full range of incident categories. Whether the time-to-detection metrics are tracked and improved.

Section B measures response. Whether response playbooks exist by incident category. Whether the playbooks are exercised in actual incidents. Whether the response containment is effective.

Section C measures investigation. Whether root cause analysis is conducted. Whether the analysis distinguishes proximate cause from underlying cause. Whether the analysis examines the systemic conditions that allowed the incident to occur.

Section D measures learning and structural change. Whether incidents drive policy revision, control redesign, risk register updates, and other structural changes. Whether the change is implemented or merely recommended. Whether the implementation is verified through subsequent operation.

Section E is the effectiveness section. Whether a structural change in the past twelve months was driven specifically by incident evidence. Privately-acknowledged incidents that should have produced structural change and did not. Predictive specificity on the incidents that would recur without the incident program. Executive alignment on incident-related accountability.

WHY THIS DIMENSION MATTERS DISPROPORTIONATELY

This dimension's importance is disproportionate to its visibility. The dimension is, at most firms, owned by an operational team that reports several levels below the executive committee. The dimension does not, in most cases, receive board attention except in response to major incidents. The dimension's contribution to governance is, however, central. The evidence about whether the governance system is working comes substantially from this dimension. Without this dimension's contribution, the other six dimensions are operating without feedback about their operational effectiveness.

Consider an analogy. A risk management function without incident learning is like a medical practice without follow-up. The diagnoses can be sophisticated. The treatments can be careful. The absence of follow-up means that the practice cannot, over time, improve. The patients who do worse than expected, the treatments that produce unexpected side effects, the diagnoses that turn out to be wrong — these are the empirical evidence that should drive the practice's improvement. Without the follow- up, the practice operates on its initial confidence, never updated against the evidence.

Governance without incident learning operates similarly. The frameworks can be elaborate. The artifacts can be impressive. The lack of feedback from incidents means that the operational effectiveness of the frameworks is not, in any reliable way, evaluated against outcomes. The frameworks continue to operate. The frameworks do not, over time, become better at producing the outcomes governance is supposed to produce.

THE MOST COMMON FINDINGS

THE DETECTION-GAP PATTERN

The first common finding is that incident detection is concentrated in technical domains and is weak in non-technical domains. Cybersecurity incidents are typically well-detected because the detection infrastructure has been built over the past decade. Operational incidents in business processes are less well-detected, because the detection infrastructure has not been built. Cultural and behavioral incidents (policy violations not detected by technical controls, ethical issues, conflicts of interest) are detected only when they reach a level of severity that surfaces them through other means.

The remediation is the extension of detection capability into the under-detected domains. The extension requires investment in monitoring infrastructure, in detection criteria, and in the staffing required to operate the extended detection. The investment is, in most cases, a Phase Two priority because it requires the broader instrumentation capability that Phase Two builds.

THE INVESTIGATION-WITHOUT-DEPTH PATTERN

The second common finding is that incident investigation stops at proximate cause. The investigation identifies what happened, when, and what immediate actions are required to remediate. It does not, in most cases, examine the systemic conditions that allowed the incident to occur. The systemic examination would reveal contributory factors in policies, controls, decision rights, training, organizational structure, or culture. The examination is rare. The remediation, without the examination, addresses the proximate cause and leaves the systemic conditions in place.

The remediation is the deepening of investigation discipline. The investigation includes the systemic examination as a routine component. The examination identifies contributory factors across the governance system. The contributory factors drive structural change in the relevant dimensions. The investigation produces, as a routine output, recommendations for structural change in policies, controls, decision rights, and other adjacent functions.

THE LEARNING-WITHOUT-IMPLEMENTATION PATTERN

The third common finding is that incident investigations produce recommendations that are not, in practice, fully implemented. The recommendations are documented. They are circulated. They are noted in the incident closure record. The implementation, when tracked, is incomplete. The implementation, when not tracked, is partial in ways the organization does not see. The recurrence rate of related incidents reveals the partial implementation. The recurrence is, at most firms, higher than the executives whose function the dimension serves would prefer to acknowledge.

The remediation is the tracking discipline. Each recommendation is assigned an owner, a deadline, and a verification mechanism. The verification confirms not only that the recommendation has been implemented but that the implementation has produced the intended effect. The tracking is operationally substantial. It is, at many firms, a missing capability.

SECTION E IN DETAIL

On structural change driven by incident evidence in the past twelve months, the dimension produces examples. The examples are sometimes substantial. The examples are also, in most cases, fewer than the incident volume would warrant. The incidents that occurred in the past twelve months should have produced more structural change than the program can document. The gap between the change that should have occurred and the change that did occur is itself diagnostic.

On privately-acknowledged incidents that should have produced structural change and did not, the dimension produces candid responses when asked seriously. The incident program team is, more often than not, aware of incidents whose structural implications were not, in the end, addressed. The implications would have required changes in functions outside the incident team's authority. The changes did not occur. The incidents recurred. The pattern is the Locked-In pattern observed through the incident dimension.

On predictive specificity regarding incidents that would recur without the program, the dimension produces more specific responses than do other dimensions. The incident team has typically conducted some analysis of incident patterns and can predict, with reasonable specificity, which categories of incident would recur with what frequency if the program were eliminated. The analysis is more developed in some incident categories than others. The variance is, again, diagnostic.

On executive alignment regarding incident-related accountability, the dimension produces particularly consequential findings. The executives associated with incidents (typically the CISO for cybersecurity, the COO for operational, the General Counsel for legal, the Head of HR for cultural) operate with substantially different views of what incident accountability means. The differences are not generally surfaced in normal executive discourse because incidents are treated as discrete events rather than as patterns that test the governance system. The assessment, conducted with separate interviews, surfaces the differences.

◆ ◆ ◆

Incident Management is the dimension that supplies the empirical evidence on which the rest of governance should adapt. At most firms, the evidence is collected and incompletely used. The incompleteness is one of the most consequential governance failures in the framework, and one of the most addressable. The Phase Three work I describe in Chapter 18 focuses substantially on the construction of the learning capability this dimension requires.

CHAPTER IN BRIEF

- Incidents are the empirical evidence about governance. The information they contain is, at most firms, not extracted: incidents are responded to and closed without the structural learning that should follow.
- The three modal patterns are: detection gap (technical incidents are well-detected, non-technical incidents are not), investigation without depth (the investigation stops at proximate cause without examining systemic conditions), and learning without implementation (recommendations are documented and circulated but not verified).
- Governance without incident learning is like a medical practice without follow-up. The frameworks can be elaborate. The lack of feedback means the frameworks cannot become better at producing the outcomes governance is supposed to produce.
- The construction of the learning capability this dimension requires is the substantial focus of the Phase Three work described in Chapter 18.

CHAPTER XI

Decision Rights and Accountability

"Authority and responsibility must travel together. When responsibility is assigned without authority, no good comes of it. When authority is assigned without responsibility, no good comes of it either. When both travel together, governance becomes possible."
— from the methodology

THE KEYSTONE

This is the dimension on which the framework's structural argument turns. The other six dimensions can be strengthened independently of one another. They produce, in isolation, partial improvements in governance. The seventh dimension is different. It is the keystone. When it is weak, the others cannot, however well-developed they are individually, produce coherent governance. When it is strong, the others can be brought into coherent operation even from positions of substantial individual weakness.

The argument I want to make in this chapter is that Decision Rights is structurally privileged in any governance framework worth the name. Not because it is more important than the others as a domain. Because the others all depend on it. A policy is operational only if there is an identifiable decision-maker whose authority the policy binds. A control is operational only if there is an identifiable decision-maker whose action the control informs. A risk is governed only if there is an identifiable decision-maker who has authority to accept or escalate it. An incident produces learning only if there is an identifiable decision-maker who can act on the learning. An AI capability is governed only if there are identifiable decision-makers across its lifecycle. A vendor is governed only if there are identifiable decision-makers whose authority over the vendor relationship is exercisable.

Decision rights are the substrate on which the other dimensions operate. When the substrate is weak, the dimensions operate on each other's documentation rather than on operational reality.

Decision rights are the substrate on which the other dimensions operate. When the substrate is weak, the dimensions operate on each other's documentation rather than on operational reality.

THE AUTHORITY MATRIX

Most large enterprises have an authority matrix. The document is typically maintained by the corporate secretary's office or the General Counsel's office. The matrix specifies which decisions can be made at which authority levels, with which approval pathways, in which amounts or categories. The matrix is, at most firms, accurate to a substantial degree for financial transactions, capital allocation, and a defined set of regulatory matters. The matrix is, in most cases, weaker for other categories of consequential decisions.

The matrix was typically authored some years ago, encoded into workflows that have, by now, calcified, and has been revised infrequently. The revisions, when they occur, are typically driven by regulatory updates, by reorganizations, or by specific incidents that surfaced the matrix's inadequacy in a particular area. The revisions are, in most cases, additive. New decision categories are added when surfaced. Existing decision categories are rarely retired. The matrix grows over time.

The matrix's accuracy is, at most firms, partial. There are categories of consequential decisions that the matrix does not address. There are categories of decisions where the matrix specifies authority that, in practice, is exercised at lower levels. There are categories where the matrix specifies authority that, in practice, no one exercises because the decision flow has bypassed the matrix's authority pathways. The matrix exists. The matrix is referenced in the policy library. The matrix is, operationally, partial.

WHERE AI HAS DISRUPTED THE MATRIX

AI has introduced categories of consequential decisions that the authority matrix, in most cases, does not address. The categories are not minor. They include: The decision to deploy an AI capability into production. Who has the authority? At many firms, this decision has been delegated to the program team that built the capability, without explicit authority delegation. The decision is made by the team that wants to deploy. The committee that nominally governs AI deployment has not, in many cases, exercised binding authority over the decision.

The decision to authorize an AI agent to take autonomous actions on the firm's behalf. The scope of the action is bounded, but the action itself is autonomous. Who has the authority to grant this autonomy? The decision rights matrix typically does not address it. The authorization is, at many firms, granted by the team operating the agent, without explicit authority.

The decision to fine-tune an AI model on firm data. The fine-tuning creates a model that, in some ways, embodies the firm's proprietary information. The fine-tuning may also produce model behavior that is harder to predict than the base model's behavior. Who has the authority to approve fine-tuning? The matrix typically does not address it.

The decision to accept the outputs of a foundation model update. The vendor pushes the update. The update changes model behavior. The firm has a window in which to evaluate the change before the update is binding. Who has the authority to accept or reject the update? The matrix typically does not address it.

The decision to allow AI to participate in customer engagements at specified levels of autonomy. The customer interaction is conducted, in part or in whole, by AI. The interactions affect the firm's customer relationships. Who has the authority to set the autonomy levels and to modify them over time? The matrix typically does not address it.

Each of these categories is a category of decisions the firm is, in 2026, making in volume. The matrix was constructed before these categories existed. The matrix has, in most cases, not been extended to cover them. The decisions are being made, in operational practice, by whichever person or team is closest to the decision when it needs to be made. The authority is, in operational reality, distributed without explicit delegation.

THE OPERATIONAL GAP

The gap between the documented authority matrix and the operational decision flow is, at most firms, the most consequential single finding the framework produces. The gap has, at firms where it is large, the following typical features: The documented matrix is current in name and out-of-date in substance. Decisions made by named authorities. In practice, decisions made by people lower in the organization, with the named authority providing nominal approval or being bypassed entirely.

The operational decision flow has its own logic, developed organically over time, often optimized for speed rather than authority. The logic includes patterns like "the team that proposes the change has the authority to make it," "the technology that enables the change is approved when it is procured," and "the new category of decision is made at the level it has historically been made, even though the new category is consequentially different from the historical category."

The named authorities, when interviewed, describe authority they believe they have. The interviewed teams, when asked separately, describe authority they actually exercise. The two accounts, brought together, reveal the gap. The gap is, in many cases, larger than either party expected. The gap is sometimes the most uncomfortable single finding the assessment produces.

WHY THE GAP IS CONSEQUENTIAL

The gap is consequential for several reasons.

Accountability is misallocated. The named authorities are nominally accountable for decisions they did not, in practice, make. The teams that made the decisions are not accountable, because they did not have the documented authority. When the decisions produce consequences, the accountability flows to the named authority who did not make the decision. The named authority experiences accountability as undeserved punishment. The team that made the decision experiences the consequences as someone else's problem. The organization does not learn from the consequences, because the learning would require addressing the gap, which the organization has not surfaced.

Decision quality is degraded. The teams that make decisions, lacking the documented authority, do not have the perspective the named authority would have brought. The teams operate on local information. The named authority would have brought broader context, broader risk perspective, and the institutional memory that the team often lacks. The decisions, made at lower levels than the matrix specifies, are made with less analytical input than the matrix's design assumed.

The matrix's authority is eroded. The matrix specifies authority that, in operational reality, is not exercised. The pattern is observed by the population the matrix bounds. The population concludes, accurately, that the matrix's specifications can be ignored without consequence. The conclusion generalizes. The matrix's authority over the decisions it does still bind is reduced. The matrix becomes, over time, decorative.

WHAT THE DIMENSION MEASURES

Section A measures matrix completeness. Coverage across decision categories, including the new AI categories. Currency against organizational and technological change.

Section B measures operational alignment. Whether the documented authority is, in practice, the operational authority. The methodology by which the alignment is verified.

Section C measures authority exercise. Whether named authorities exercise their authority when warranted, including the authority to decline or escalate.

Section D measures accountability fidelity. Whether accountability for decisions, when consequences materialize, flows to the parties who actually made the decisions.

Section E is the effectiveness section. Whether a structural change to the authority matrix in the past twelve months was driven specifically by evidence from the dimension's operation. Privately- acknowledged gaps the program cannot escalate. Predictive specificity on the consequences of the matrix being weakened. Executive alignment on the dimension's purpose.

WHAT MATURE PRACTICE LOOKS LIKE

Stage 3 in this dimension means the matrix is current, covers the major decision categories, and is referenced in the relevant policies. Most large enterprises operate at Stage 3 for traditional financial and operational decisions, with weaker coverage for AI and other newer categories.

Stage 4 requires the matrix to be operationally exercised. The named authorities actually make the decisions the matrix specifies. The operational decision flow matches the documented authority. The teams operating under the matrix understand their authority and exercise it within the bounded scope. The integration with the other dimensions is operational: the policies, controls, and risk acceptance pathways reference the matrix, and the matrix is consistent with what they reference.

Stage 5 requires the matrix to be alive. Decisions made under the matrix produce evidence about the matrix's operational quality. The evidence drives revisions to the matrix. New decision categories that emerge through technological change or organizational change are surfaced and added to the matrix. Decision categories whose authority no longer corresponds to the decision's actual consequence are revised. The matrix is, over time, a continuously updated artifact rather than a periodic artifact.

THE MOST COMMON FINDINGS

THE AI-DECISION-CATEGORY-GAP PATTERN

The first common finding is that the authority matrix does not address the AI-specific decision categories described earlier in this chapter. The matrix was constructed before these categories existed. The matrix has not been extended. The decisions are being made, in operational practice, without documented authority. The matrix extension is, an immediate Phase One priority in the advisory work this framework is designed to support.

THE OPERATIONAL-REALITY-GAP PATTERN

The second common finding is that the matrix's specified authority is, in many decision categories, not the operational authority. The gap is sometimes large. The gap is more often medium-sized but consequential. The named authority believes they have authority they do not, in practice, exercise. The teams that make decisions believe they have authority that the matrix does not, in practice, document. The gap is the consequential finding.

THE ACCOUNTABILITY-MISMATCH PATTERN

The third common finding is that, when decisions produce consequences, the accountability flows to parties other than those who actually made the decisions. The mismatch is sometimes the structural punishment of the named authority. The mismatch is sometimes the diffusion of accountability to the point that no one is, in practice, accountable. Either failure produces dysfunction. The first produces named authorities who become risk-averse and decline to delegate even authority they ought to. The second produces decisions made by no one identifiable, with consequences that no one bears.

SECTION E IN DETAIL

The effectiveness section in this dimension produces, in practice, the most consequential findings the assessment generates.

On evidence-driven matrix revision in the past twelve months, the dimension typically produces no examples. The matrix has been revised in some way. The revisions are typically driven by organizational change or by external requirement. Revisions driven by evidence from the matrix's own operation (decisions that produced bad outcomes and revealed inadequacies in the authority) are uncommon. The absence is itself the finding.

On privately-acknowledged authority gaps that cannot be escalated, the dimension produces lists when asked under conditions of candor. The teams operating under the matrix can identify, in most cases, authority categories where the matrix's specifications are routinely bypassed and where the bypass has been institutionalized to the point that escalating it would be considered impolite. The bypass is well- known within the operational layer of the firm and has, in most cases, not been raised to the executive layer.

On predictive specificity regarding the consequences of the matrix being weakened, the dimension produces generic responses. The matrix's value is asserted in abstract terms. The specific consequences of a weakened matrix are not, in most cases, articulated with the specificity that a Stage 5 organization would produce.

On executive alignment regarding the dimension's purpose, the dimension produces particularly consequential findings. The executives associated with the matrix (CEO, General Counsel, corporate secretary) operate with substantially different views of what the matrix is for. Some view the matrix as a compliance instrument. Some view it as an operational instrument. Some view it as a defensive instrument that exists to allocate accountability after the fact. The differences are not generally surfaced in normal executive discourse, and the differences shape, in non-obvious ways, the matrix's actual operation.

WHY THIS IS THE KEYSTONE

I have argued that Decision Rights is the keystone dimension. The argument is structural and operational rather than rhetorical.

Structurally, the other six dimensions all depend on decision rights. A policy without an identifiable decision-maker whose behavior it binds is decorative. A control without an identifiable decision-maker whose action it informs is operationally vacant. A risk without an identifiable decision-maker who can accept or escalate it is unmanaged. An incident without an identifiable decision-maker who can act on its lessons is wasted. An AI capability without identifiable decision-makers across its lifecycle is ungoverned. A vendor without identifiable decision-makers whose authority over the relationship is exercisable is, in operational reality, the vendor's decision rather than the customer's.

Each of the other dimensions can be operationally strong only when the underlying decision rights are operationally strong. When the decision rights are weak, the other dimensions can produce documentation, artifacts, and apparent operation. They cannot produce coherent governance. The documentation is referencing decision authority that does not, in practice, exist. The artifacts are produced by people whose authority to produce them is not, in practice, exercised. The apparent operation is operating in parallel to the actual decision flow.

Operationally, the work to strengthen Decision Rights is the work that, once done, makes the other work possible. Without it, the other work is dressing up artifacts. With it, the other work is constructing governance. The sequencing implications of this position are the substance of Chapter 15.

THE SPECIFIC CONSEQUENCES FOR PHASE ONE

The argument that Decision Rights is the keystone has direct implications for what the work to remediate enterprise governance should begin with. Specifically, Phase One of the remediation focuses substantially on Decision Rights. The other dimensions receive attention, but the focus of attention is here.

The Phase One work in this dimension includes: The extension of the authority matrix to cover the AI-specific decision categories. The categories are, by 2026, well-defined enough that the extension can be done with reasonable confidence.

The verification of operational alignment. The matrix is examined against operational reality. The gaps are identified. The gaps are addressed through either matrix revision (to match operational practice where the practice is acceptable) or operational change (to match the matrix where the matrix's specifications are appropriate).

The exercise of authority where it has been delegated downward without documentation. The named authorities, who have allowed their authority to be exercised at lower levels for operational reasons, take back the authority and exercise it. The exercise requires the operational mechanisms that allow the authority to operate at the speed the operations require. The mechanisms are part of the Phase One construction.

The alignment of accountability with decision-making. Accountability for decisions, when consequences materialize, flows to the parties who made the decisions. The flow requires the documentation that the decisions were made and by whom. The documentation is part of the Phase One construction.

Phase One is roughly six months of focused work. The work is consequential. The work is also, in my experience, the work most enterprises have been deferring. The deferral is the central finding of the assessment when the assessment reveals the Decision Rights dimension at Stage 2 or below. The deferral is what produces the governance dysfunction that the other dimensions reflect. The remediation begins here.

◆ ◆ ◆

Decision Rights is the keystone. The remaining chapters in this part will not return to it as the primary subject, because the framework's dimensional walk-through is now complete. The argument about the keystone runs through the rest of the book in different ways. Part Three describes the diagnostic patterns the framework produces, several of which surface decision rights findings indirectly. Part Four describes the sequenced work the patterns warrant, with Decision Rights as the Phase One focus.

CHAPTER IN BRIEF

- Decision Rights is the keystone dimension. The other six can be strengthened independently and produce partial improvements. The keystone is different: when it is weak, the others cannot produce coherent governance. When it is strong, the others can be brought into coherent operation even from positions of substantial individual weakness.
- The authority matrix at most enterprises does not address the AI-specific decision categories that have emerged since the matrix was authored. The decisions are being made, in operational practice, without documented authority.
- The gap between documented authority and operational reality is, at firms where it is large, the most consequential single finding the framework produces. It produces accountability misallocation, decision quality degradation, and the gradual erosion of the matrix's authority over time.
- Phase One of the remediation focuses substantially on this dimension. The matrix is extended to cover AI decisions; the operational alignment is verified; the authority is exercised where it has been informally delegated; and accountability is aligned with actual decision-making.

PART THREE

The Diagnosis

How four cumulative patterns emerge from the framework, what each indicates about the organization's actual condition, and how to read your own organization through them.

CHAPTER XII

The Signature Element

"The patterns are not in the data. They are in what the data refuses to do."

— from an internal methodology note

Every dimension in the framework has a fifth section. Sections A through D measure structure and operation. Section E measures something different. It measures effectiveness. The distinction is not rhetorical. The two kinds of measurement produce different findings. Structure and operation can be strong while effectiveness is weak. The form-substance gap is visible only when both are measured.

This chapter is about Section E specifically. The signature element. The diagnostic instrument that, applied with consistent logic across dimensions, surfaces what conventional governance assessments leave undisclosed.

I have come to think the signature element is the most analytically powerful component of the framework. The dimension structures are useful. The five-stage scale is useful. The floor and gap rules are useful. The signature element is what distinguishes the framework from a thorough but ordinary maturity model. The element does diagnostic work that, in my experience, no other governance assessment instrument does at this level of specificity.

WHAT THE SIGNATURE ELEMENT SURFACES

LEARNING VERSUS BEING DRIVEN

The signature element distinguishes responsive programs from learning programs. A responsive program changes when something outside it prompts the change. A regulator issues a directive. An audit produces a finding. An executive imposes a requirement. The change occurs in response to the external prompt. The program is operating; it is also being driven.

A learning program changes when its own evidence indicates that change is warranted. The program's operation produces information about its own effectiveness. The information triggers structural revision. The change is driven by the program's analytical capability rather than by external prompting. The learning program is, in important ways, qualitatively different from the responsive program. The learning program improves over time. The responsive program operates.

THE LOCKED-IN CONDITION

The Locked-In condition is characteristic of governance programs that have lost the capacity to change what they know is not working. The program team has accurate diagnostic capability about its own dysfunction. The team also lacks the authority, the political position, or the will to address what the diagnosis reveals. The combination produces persistent dysfunction that the team understands and cannot, in practice, change.

Surfacing the condition requires conditions of confidentiality to be answered honestly. Under normal conditions, the program team will not surface privately-acknowledged ineffectiveness, because the surfacing implicates the team in continuing to operate something they know to be ineffective. The interview methodology has to construct conditions under which the candor is possible. The candor, once available, produces findings that conventional assessments do not.

THE UNMODELED CONDITION

The Unmodeled condition is what governance functions exhibit when they assert value but cannot articulate it. A program that contributes value should be able to articulate the value with specificity. Specific risks that would materialize. Specific decisions that would be made worse. Specific consequences that would follow. The articulation requires the program to have done the analytical work of modeling its own contribution.

Many programs have not done the analytical work. The programs operate. The contribution to governance is asserted in abstract terms. The specific contribution is not articulated, because the analytical work of articulating it has not been undertaken. The program may be contributing value. The program may not be. The absence of the articulation makes the determination impossible.

THE MISALIGNED CONDITION

The Misaligned condition is produced by senior-executive divergence that the organization has not surfaced. Senior executives operating in the same organization can have substantially different views of what a governance function is for, what risks it should mitigate, and what success would look like. The differences are not generally surfaced in normal executive discourse, because the topic is treated abstractly and the discourse is brief. The differences shape, in non-obvious ways, the function's actual operation. The function is, in many cases, optimizing for one executive's view while the other executives expect it to be optimizing for theirs.

The condition is only surfaced through separate interviews with the named executives. The interviews are part of the engagement methodology. The findings are produced by the comparison across the interviews rather than by any single interview.

WHY THESE FOUR FAILURE MODES

The four diagnostic axes are not, in their selection, arbitrary. They reflect the failure modes that are most common in governance functions, as the failure modes appear in the work that has informed this framework. The functions fail in identifiable ways. The four axes correspond to the four failure modes most worth surfacing.

The first failure mode is operating without learning. The function is doing what it does. The function is not improving. The function will continue to operate in approximately its current form until external prompting requires it to change. The signature element surfaces this.

The second failure mode is operating with known dysfunction. The function contains components the team knows to be ineffective. The components persist because the political work of changing them has not been undertaken. The Locked-In condition is what this looks like in operation.

The third failure mode is operating without analytical clarity. The function contributes value, or believes it does, but cannot articulate the contribution with specificity. The lack of articulation prevents the function from optimizing its own contribution. The function operates on its initial design, never updated against the evidence of what it actually contributes. The Unmodeled condition is the name for this failure mode.

The fourth failure mode is operating with senior misalignment. The named executives expect different things from the function. The function cannot satisfy all the expectations. The function satisfies some, fails others, and operates in a chronic state of being held to incompatible standards. The Misaligned condition is the name for this failure mode.

Other failure modes exist. The four I have selected are the ones that, in my experience, are most common, most consequential, and most addressable. Surfaced, they become tractable. Unsurfaced, they remain operative and undiscussed.

HOW THE SIGNATURE ELEMENT IS APPLIED

The signature element is applied across all seven dimensions with the same underlying structure but in dimension-specific translation. What evidence-driven change looks like in the Policy dimension is different from what it looks like in the Controls or Risk dimensions, and the diagnostic instrument is calibrated accordingly. The substance of what is being asked is consistent across dimensions; the specificity is dimension-dependent.

The signature element draws from two distinct interview sources. The program team responsible for the dimension is interviewed about the function's operation and its honest assessment of that operation.

The named senior executives are interviewed separately. The findings emerge from the triangulation across the two sources rather than from either source alone.

Most enterprises produce, on the signature element, findings that cluster at the lower end of the maturity scale across dimensions. Some dimensions perform worse than others. Few perform better. The accumulated findings across the seven dimensions produce the diagnostic patterns that the next chapter describes.

WHY CONVENTIONAL ASSESSMENTS MISS THIS

Conventional governance assessments focus on structure and operation. The dimension is structured. The dimension is operating. The conventional assessment produces a passing finding. The signature element asks different questions. The questions are not, in their substance, novel. Practitioners with experience in governance functions would recognize the questions as the questions they ask themselves privately. The questions are asked, in the framework, formally and on the record. The formality changes the answers.

Specifically, the formality changes the answers in two ways. First, the formality requires the program team to articulate answers they may have left unarticulated. The articulation produces clarity that the program team did not previously have. Second, the formality compares answers across interview subjects, which surfaces misalignments that the subjects had not previously seen. The two changes — internal articulation and cross-interview comparison — produce the diagnostic findings that the signature element generates.

The findings are uncomfortable. The findings are also productive. The discomfort is the precondition for the structural change that the findings indicate. The organization that receives uncomfortable findings has, in the receiving, taken the first step toward addressing them. The organization that receives comfortable findings has, in the receiving, confirmed that the assessment was not, in fact, diagnostic.

> *An assessment whose findings are entirely comfortable for the organization to receive is, in most cases, not telling the organization anything it did not already know.*

◆ ◆ ◆

The signature element is the analytical machinery that produces the patterns. The next chapter describes the patterns themselves. The patterns are the diagnostic categories that emerge across dimensions and across the diagnostic axes the signature element interrogates. The patterns are what makes the framework's output more useful than the dimension scores alone would be.

CHAPTER IN BRIEF

- Every dimension has a Section E that measures effectiveness rather than structure and operation. The signature element interrogates four diagnostic axes that surface what conventional governance assessments leave undisclosed.
- The signature element is designed to surface four failure modes that conventional assessments miss: operating without learning, operating with known dysfunction, operating without analytical clarity, and operating with senior misalignment.
- The signature element is applied across all seven dimensions in dimension-specific translation. The findings emerge from triangulation across program-team interviews, separate executive interviews, and documentary evidence.
- Conventional assessments focus on structure and operation. The signature element asks different questions. The formality of the asking, and the comparison across interview subjects, produces diagnostic findings that conventional assessments cannot.

CHAPTER XIII

The Four Cumulative Patterns

"Most pathologies announce themselves clearly when you know what to listen for."
— from the methodology

Across the work in which the framework has been applied, the signature element has produced findings that cluster into four diagnostic patterns. The patterns are cumulative. They emerge in approximately the order presented here, with later patterns typically appearing only in organizations that have first developed the earlier ones. The cumulative structure is important. Recognizing it allows the assessment to predict not only the current state but the trajectory the organization has been on and the direction it is, without intervention, likely to continue.

This chapter describes the four patterns: Documentation Theater, Locked-In, Unmodeled, and Misaligned. Each is named for the operational condition it describes. Each can be recognized by the specific findings that surface it. Each carries implications for the work the organization should undertake to address it.

PATTERN ONE: DOCUMENTATION THEATER

The first pattern is the one most enterprises develop, and the one that most organizations either have already developed or are in the process of developing. The pattern is structural. The organization produces governance documentation in volume. The documentation is, at the surface, impressive. The documentation also exceeds the operational governance that the documentation describes. The gap between the documentation and the operation is the pattern's central feature.

Documentation Theater is, in operational reality, the substitution of artifact production for governance work. The artifacts include policies, procedures, control documentation, risk registers, AI inventories, incident response playbooks, vendor risk assessments, and audit findings. The artifacts are real. They are produced by people with the skill to produce them. They satisfy the audiences that evaluate them. The audiences include auditors, regulators, board members, and external assessors. The audiences are not, in most cases, in a position to evaluate whether the artifacts correspond to operational reality.

The pattern develops in several typical ways. The most common pathway is that the organization invested heavily in compliance after a regulatory event (Sarbanes-Oxley, a major incident, a regulatory finding) and continued the investment afterward without recalibrating the investment to the operational state. The compliance machinery, once stood up, persisted. The documentation continued to be produced. The operational gap, never substantially addressed, persisted alongside.

The pattern is diagnosed by Section A and Section C findings that are substantially stronger than Section D and Section E findings across multiple dimensions. The structure is present. The communication is operating. The actual enforcement, monitoring, and learning are weak. The pattern is, in its mature form, observable in nearly every dimension simultaneously, because the underlying organizational dynamics that produce it are not specific to any one function.

Documentation Theater is, in operational reality, the precondition for the other three patterns. An organization that does not produce Documentation Theater would generally not develop the other patterns, because the conditions that produce the other patterns include the documentation-heavy operating mode that Theater produces. Theater is the substrate.

PATTERN TWO: LOCKED-IN

The second pattern emerges on the substrate of the first. The organization has developed substantial governance documentation. The documentation reflects, in part, governance decisions made by senior executives whose positions in the organization are persistent. The decisions have been encoded into the documentation, into the workflows, and into the operational culture. The decisions have, over time, become difficult to revise.

The Locked-In pattern is the persistence of governance components that the program teams privately believe to be ineffective. The components might be policies that no one observes, controls that operate without effect, risk register items that have not been updated in years, vendor relationships that have outlived their value, AI capabilities that the firm wishes it had not deployed, incident processes that consistently produce recommendations no one implements, decision rights that have been bypassed for so long the bypass has become the operational reality.

The components persist because their removal would require political work the organization has not undertaken. The senior executive who originally sponsored the component is still in place. The institutional memory of why the component was created has been lost, and the people who could remove it cannot get authorization from anyone whose authorization would be sufficient. The component continues to operate. The team knows it is ineffective. The team continues to operate it.

The pattern is diagnosed through the signature element's interrogation of privately-acknowledged ineffectiveness across dimensions. The accumulated findings, where the program teams candidly surface dysfunction they cannot change, produce the Locked-In diagnosis. The diagnosis is, where Documentation Theater is observed, accompanied by the Locked-In diagnosis at lower amplitude.

The Locked-In pattern varies substantially in its severity from organization to organization. Some organizations have one or two Locked-In components per dimension. Some organizations have many. The cumulative load of

Locked-In components is itself diagnostic. Organizations carrying many Locked-In components are operating substantial governance overhead that is not contributing to governance outcomes. The overhead is consuming resources, executive attention, and political capital that could be allocated to governance work that would, in fact, contribute.

PATTERN THREE: UNMODELED

The third pattern emerges on the substrate of the first two. The organization has substantial documentation and known dysfunction. The organization also has, in many of its governance functions, no analytical capability for modeling its own contribution. The function exists. The function operates. The specific value the function contributes is not, in most cases, articulated with the specificity that would allow the function to be optimized.

The Unmodeled pattern is the absence of operational specificity about what the governance function contributes. The function asserts contribution in abstract terms. The function cannot, when asked, articulate the specific risks that would materialize without it, the specific decisions that would be made worse, or the specific consequences that would follow. The function is operating on the assumption that it contributes value. The assumption may be correct. The lack of analytical articulation prevents the assumption from being tested.

The pattern is diagnosed through the signature element's interrogation of predictive specificity across dimensions. The generic responses to specificity-demanding probes, accumulated across dimensions, produce the Unmodeled diagnosis. The diagnosis is, where Documentation Theater is observed, accompanied by the Unmodeled diagnosis.

The Unmodeled pattern has consequences beyond the specific functions that exhibit it. An organization whose governance functions are substantially Unmodeled cannot optimize its governance investment. The organization cannot, in any defensible way, decide whether to invest more in one function or another. The investment decisions are made on the basis of organizational politics, recent incidents, or executive preference. The investment decisions are not made on the basis of analytical evidence about which functions contribute most. The cumulative effect is that governance investment is poorly allocated. The poor allocation persists because the analytical capability to improve it has not been constructed.

PATTERN FOUR: MISALIGNED

The fourth pattern emerges on the substrate of the first three. The organization has substantial documentation, known dysfunction, and unmodeled functions. The organization also has, at the senior executive level, substantial misalignment about what governance is for and what it should produce. The misalignment is not, in most cases, visible at the surface of executive discourse. The executives talk about governance in general terms. The general terms accommodate substantially different views. The differences shape, in non-obvious ways, the function's actual operation.

The Misaligned pattern is the persistent state of being held to incompatible standards by different senior executives. The function is told, by the CEO, to be strategic. The function is told, by the CRO, to be cautious. The function is told, by the General Counsel, to be defensive. The function is told, by the chief audit executive, to be evidentiable. The standards are not, in all cases, compatible. The function cannot satisfy all of them. The function satisfies some, fails others, and operates in chronic tension. The tension is itself a governance failure mode that the framework explicitly surfaces.

The pattern is diagnosed through the signature element's interrogation of executive alignment, performed via separate executive interviews and cross-interview comparison. The misalignments, accumulated across dimensions, produce the Misaligned diagnosis.

CASE IN POINT

THREE EXECUTIVES, THREE DEFINITIONS, ONE AI PROGRAM

A mid-sized technology company asked me to review its AI governance program. The CEO, the CRO, and the General Counsel each requested a one-hour interview as part of the engagement. I conducted the interviews on consecutive days, without sharing any executive's responses with the others. The substantive question I asked each was the same: what is the AI governance program for, and what would success look like in twenty- four months?

The CEO's answer was acceleration. The program existed to ensure that the company could deploy AI capabilities faster than competitors. Success was measured in the number of customer-facing AI features released per quarter, the time from AI capability identification to production deployment, and the company's competitive position in the AI-enabled subsegments of its market. Governance was the mechanism that made speed possible without creating intolerable risk.

The CRO's answer was risk reduction. The program existed to ensure that the AI the company deployed did not produce material adverse events. Success was measured in the absence of significant AI incidents, the maturity of monitoring and response capabilities, and the demonstrability of the firm's risk posture to regulators and customers. Governance was the mechanism that made AI deployment defensible.

The General Counsel's answer was litigation defense. The program existed to ensure that, when AI-related claims arose, the company had documented governance that would withstand discovery and trial. Success was measured in the defensibility of the AI-related documentation, the rigor of the approval workflows, and the alignment with emerging regulatory expectations. Governance was the mechanism that made AI deployment legally durable.

None of the three answers was wrong. All three were partial. The AI governance program had been operating, for three years, in chronic tension between the three. The tension had shaped what the program produced. The team had concluded, sensibly enough, that the safest path was to satisfy the documentation requirements that all three executives could agree on, and to defer the substantive choices among the three views to later. The deferred choices had become, over time, the program's central limitation. The program was running. The program was not, in any direct sense, fulfilling any of the three executive expectations of it.

The Misaligned pattern is, when it surfaces, the most consequential of the four. The pattern indicates that the organization is operating without senior executive alignment on what the governance functions are for. The functions cannot, in this condition, be optimized. The functions cannot be appropriately resourced. The functions cannot be appropriately measured. The lack of alignment is, in many ways, the structural condition that prevents the organization from addressing the other three patterns. Until the executives are aligned, the work to address Documentation Theater, Locked-In, and Unmodeled cannot proceed coherently, because the work would require choices about what governance is for, and the choices cannot be made without alignment.

WHY THE PATTERNS ARE CUMULATIVE

I have asserted that the patterns are cumulative. Each later pattern emerges only in organizations that have first developed the earlier patterns. The argument is empirical rather than theoretical. In the work that informs this framework, I have not seen Locked-In without Documentation Theater, Unmodeled without Locked-In, or Misaligned without Unmodeled. The patterns appear in the cumulative order, with later patterns appearing only in organizations that have first developed the earlier patterns.

The theoretical argument for the cumulative structure is also defensible, though it is not the basis for the claim. The argument is that the conditions that produce each pattern require the conditions that produce the prior pattern. Locked-In requires substantial documentation, because the locked-in components must be specifiable. Unmodeled requires the operational complexity that documentation produces, because the analytical work of modeling is required to manage the complexity. Misaligned requires the operational complexity to surface the misalignments, which are typically masked at lower levels of complexity.

The cumulative structure has implications for diagnosis. The presence of a later pattern implies the presence of the earlier patterns. An organization that is Misaligned has, almost certainly, Documentation Theater, Locked-In components, and Unmodeled functions. An organization that is Unmodeled has, almost certainly, Documentation Theater and Locked-In components. The diagnosis of a later pattern is partial diagnosis of the earlier patterns.

The cumulative structure also has implications for remediation. The remediation, in most cases, must proceed in the order the patterns emerged. The Misaligned condition cannot be addressed without first addressing the Unmodeled condition. The Unmodeled condition cannot be addressed without first addressing the Locked-In condition. The Locked-In condition cannot be addressed without first addressing the Documentation Theater condition. The remediation has a structural sequencing that the patterns themselves indicate.

◆ ◆ ◆

The next chapter describes how to read your own organization through these patterns. The chapter is intended for executives who have read this far and are wondering what the diagnosis would be for their own firm. The answer depends on what the assessment would actually reveal, but there are signals available in advance that can be read with reasonable accuracy by an honest observer.

CHAPTER IN BRIEF

- Four cumulative patterns emerge from the signature element: Documentation Theater (substantial documentation that exceeds operational governance), Locked-In (components the team privately believes ineffective but cannot remove), Unmodeled (operational specificity absent on what the program contributes), and Misaligned (senior executives hold substantially different views of what governance is for).
- The patterns are cumulative. Later patterns appear only in organizations that have first developed the earlier ones. The presence of Misaligned implies the presence of the other three.
- Documentation Theater is the substrate. Locked-In is the persistence of known dysfunction. Unmodeled is the absence of analytical clarity. Misaligned is the absence of senior executive alignment.
- The cumulative structure has remediation implications. The patterns must be addressed in approximately the order they emerged. Misaligned cannot be addressed without first addressing Unmodeled; Unmodeled without Locked-In; Locked-In without Documentation Theater.

CHAPTER XIV

Reading Your Own Organization

"The most useful diagnostic question is the one the organization has been avoiding."
— from the methodology

The framework is designed to be applied through structured assessment. The assessment produces findings of substance. The methodology, the interview discipline, the cross-source triangulation, and the analytical capability to recognize the patterns are not, in any meaningful way, available to executives reading this book on a Sunday afternoon.

That said, the patterns the framework surfaces are not invisible without the formal assessment. The patterns have signals that can be read by an honest executive who knows what to look for. The signals are not, on their own, sufficient for diagnosis. The signals are sufficient for orientation. An executive who reads the signals accurately can know, with reasonable confidence, what the formal assessment would substantially confirm.

This chapter is about how to read the signals. It is intended for executives who have read this far and are wondering what the diagnosis would be for their own firm. The chapter is the bridge between the framework's diagnostic structure and the executive's lived experience of their own organization.

READING DOCUMENTATION THEATER

Documentation Theater has visible signals. The signals are not, on their own, definitive. They are diagnostic in their accumulation.

Signal one: the size of the policy library. If the library has more than a few hundred policies, and if the executive cannot, off the top of their head, name what a randomly-selected ten policies are about, the library has likely exceeded operational governance. The library is a sign of investment in documentation. The investment may or may not correspond to operational binding.

Signal two: the recency of policy revision. If most policies are revised on their documented revision schedule and few policies have been revised in response to specific operational evidence, the library is operating on a maintenance cadence rather than an improvement cadence. The maintenance is what Documentation Theater produces.

Signal three: the relationship between the audit findings and the management response. If the audit findings consistently produce management responses that document the existing controls and commit to no structural change, the audit-response cycle is producing artifact rather than improvement. The artifact production is what Theater is.

Signal four: the volume of governance reporting. If the executive committee reviews governance reporting that runs to many slides per quarter, and if the substantive discussion of governance during the executive committee meetings is brief, the reporting volume is exceeding the substantive engagement. The volume is the Theater. The brevity of substantive discussion is the indication that the Theater is operating as Theater.

Signal five: the relationship between governance investment and incident reduction. If governance investment has been substantial over multiple years and incident rates have been stable or rising, the governance investment is not, in operational reality, reducing the incidents the investment was supposed to reduce. The continued investment despite the absence of incident reduction is what Theater looks like in motion.

Each signal, on its own, can have benign explanations. Multiple signals together are diagnostic. An organization exhibiting several of these signals simultaneously has, with high probability, the Documentation Theater pattern in some form.

READING LOCKED-IN

Locked-In is harder to read from outside the program team. The signals are less visible at the executive level, because the privately-acknowledged ineffectiveness is, by definition, not surfaced publicly.

Signal one: persistent areas the program team avoids discussing in detail. If, when the executive asks the program team about a specific component of the program, the team produces general responses that decline to engage with the specifics, the avoidance is itself diagnostic. The team has, in most cases, accurate knowledge that they have decided not to share with the executive. The decision is rarely overt. The team has concluded that surfacing the knowledge would be unproductive, given the political dynamics. The avoidance is the operational consequence of that conclusion.

Signal two: program components whose existence is justified by reference to historical decisions. If the team explains why a component exists by reference to a decision made by an executive who has since left the firm, by reference to a regulatory event that has been substantially overtaken by subsequent events, or by reference to institutional memory that no one alive in the firm directly possesses, the component may be Locked-In. The historical justification is, in many cases, a sign that the current justification has not been examined.

Signal three: components that have not been substantively reviewed for retirement. If the executive asks the program team when a specific component was last considered for retirement, and the team cannot identify a recent consideration, the component may be Locked-In. The absence of consideration is, in most cases, a sign that the component's persistence is the path of least political resistance, regardless of its operational contribution.

READING UNMODELED

Unmodeled has direct executive signals. The signals can be read with relatively high confidence.

Signal one: the program's response to elimination questions. If the executive asks the program leader to articulate, with operational specificity, what would happen if the program were eliminated, and the response is in abstract terms (risks would materialize, decisions would be worse, consequences would follow), the program is, with high probability, Unmodeled. The specific articulation requires analytical work the program has not undertaken.

Signal two: the program's response to investment-allocation questions. If the executive asks the program leader to articulate which program component contributes the most value per dollar of investment, and the response is unspecific, the program has not done the analytical work of differentiating its components by value contribution. The investment allocation is being made on grounds other than analytical value.

Signal three: the program's response to comparison questions. If the executive asks how the program's contribution compares to peer benchmark programs, and the response is anecdotal rather than analytical, the program does not have the analytical capability to position its own contribution. The comparison capability is part of what modeling the contribution requires.

READING MISALIGNED

Misaligned has the most visible executive signals, available to any executive who attends executive committee meetings with reasonable attention.

Signal one: the divergence in executive committee discussion of governance topics. If, when governance topics are discussed in the executive committee, different executives raise different concerns, and the concerns do not appear to be working toward a common understanding, the executives are not, on the topic, aligned. The lack of alignment is, in most cases, persistent. The lack persists because the alignment work has not been undertaken.

Signal two: the divergence in executive committee priorities. If, when the governance function is asked to prioritize across competing demands, different executives express different priorities, and the priorities have not been reconciled at the executive committee level, the function is operating in conditions of chronic Misalignment. The reconciliation work is what Misalignment remediation requires.

Signal three: the divergence in executive committee evaluation of governance outcomes. If, when governance outcomes are reviewed, different executives evaluate the same outcomes differently, the executives are operating with substantially different criteria for what governance success looks like.

The criteria are not, in most cases, made explicit. The lack of explicitness is what allows the Misalignment to persist undiscussed.

WHAT TO DO WITH THE READING

An executive who reads the signals and arrives at a tentative diagnosis is in a position to take three kinds of action.

The first is to seek the formal assessment. The assessment will substantially confirm or substantially refine the tentative diagnosis. The confirmation produces actionable specificity. The refinement produces accuracy that the executive reading alone cannot provide. The assessment costs less than most executives expect and produces output that justifies the cost in nearly every case.

The second is to begin internal preparation for the assessment. The preparation is not, primarily, about gathering documentation. It is about preparing the executive team for the conversation the assessment will produce. The assessment surfaces findings that, in most cases, the executive team has not collectively addressed. The preparation includes the establishment of conditions under which the findings can be received, processed, and acted on. The conditions include, at minimum, an executive sponsor with the authority to act on what the assessment surfaces and the political position to override the resistance the findings will produce.

The third is to begin the Phase One work described in Chapter 16. The work is the work the diagnosis indicates is most consequential. The work can be begun without the formal assessment, on the basis of the executive's tentative reading. The work, begun in this way, produces some structural improvement and substantial preparation for the more rigorous work that the formal assessment enables. Beginning without the assessment is not optimal. It is, however, better than not beginning.

◆ ◆ ◆

The framework's diagnostic output is the input to the remediation work. The remediation is structured in three phases, organized around the keystone principle described in Chapter 11. The next part of the book is about the phases, beginning with the sequencing logic that determines which work belongs in which phase.

CHAPTER IN BRIEF

- The patterns the framework surfaces have signals that can be read by an honest executive who knows what to look for. The reading does not substitute for the formal assessment, but it produces orientation that is, in most cases, substantially accurate.
- Documentation Theater has five readable signals: oversized policy library, schedule-driven revision cadence, audit-response patterns that produce artifact rather than change, high volume of governance reporting, and persistent investment without incident reduction.
- Locked-In is harder to read from outside the program team. The signals include components the team avoids discussing in detail, components justified by reference to historical decisions, and components that have not been substantively reviewed for retirement.
- Unmodeled has direct executive signals: generic responses to elimination questions, unspecific responses to investment-allocation questions, anecdotal responses to comparison questions. Misaligned is the most visible: divergent executive committee discussions, priorities, and outcome evaluations.

PART FOUR

The Work

The three-phase remediation logic, the sequencing principle that governs it, and what the executives who undertake it can expect.

CHAPTER XV

Sequencing and the Keystone Principle

"The order of operations is, in most consequential work, the difference between progress and the appearance of progress."
— from the methodology

The framework produces a current-state diagnosis. The diagnosis is, in practice, more uncomfortable than the executives commissioning the assessment expected. The natural response, when the diagnosis is received, is to want to address all the findings at once. The response is, in most cases, the wrong response.

The remediation work the framework recommends is sequenced. The sequencing is not arbitrary. It reflects the dependencies between dimensions, the cumulative structure of the diagnostic patterns, and the keystone principle that places Decision Rights at the structural center. This chapter is about the sequencing logic. It explains why the work is organized in three phases, what each phase produces, and what the consequences are of attempting the work in a different order.

THREE PHASES

The remediation work is organized in three phases. Phase One addresses the keystone. Phase Two operationalizes governance across the operating dimensions. Phase Three constructs the learning systems that the framework's Stage 5 requires.

The phases are not equal in duration. Phase One runs approximately six months. Phase Two runs approximately twelve months. Phase Three runs approximately eighteen months. The total duration of all three phases is roughly three years from initiation. The phases overlap. Phase Two begins before Phase One is complete. Phase Three begins before Phase Two is complete. The overlap is operational rather than logical. The logic of the phases is sequential. The execution is staggered.

Phase One is the work I have argued is the keystone work. The work focuses on Decision Rights. The authority matrix is extended to cover the new categories of AI decisions. The operational alignment between the documented matrix and the actual decision flow is established. The named authorities exercise the authority the matrix specifies. The accountability for decisions, when consequences materialize, flows to the parties who made the decisions. The phase produces the structural foundation on which the rest of the work depends.

Phase Two operationalizes the governance functions across the operating dimensions. The dimension- specific work is substantial. Policies are reviewed against operational evidence and revised where the evidence indicates they should be. Controls are reviewed against demonstrable effectiveness and retired or redesigned where the evidence indicates they should be. Risk identification is calibrated against materialized risks. Vendor risk is extended for AI-specific considerations. AI Use and Lifecycle governance is built out across the components the dimension requires. Incident management is deepened to produce structural learning.

Phase Three constructs the learning systems. The systems make the governance dimensions, in operation, capable of improving themselves. The systems include the analytical capability that the Unmodeled pattern requires for remediation. The systems include the integration between dimensions that allows evidence from one dimension to drive structural change in another. The systems include the executive-level alignment work that the Misaligned pattern requires for remediation. Phase Three is the work that produces Stage 5 governance, where the governance is, in operation, generating evidence about its own effectiveness and updating itself in response.

WHY PHASE ONE COMES FIRST

Phase One must come first. The keystone principle requires it. The operating dimensions can be operationally strong only when the underlying decision rights are operationally strong. The work to strengthen the operating dimensions is, when undertaken before the keystone work, producing documentation rather than governance. The documentation describes decision authority that does not, in practice, exist. The work, however well-executed, accumulates artifact without operational consequence.

The argument is not theoretical. The empirical observation, from the work that informs this framework, is that organizations that have attempted to strengthen the operating dimensions without first strengthening the keystone produce limited improvement. The artifacts improve. The operational governance does not, substantially, improve. The cumulative investment in Phase Two work, conducted without Phase One foundation, produces governance that looks better on paper without operating better in practice.

The argument also has implications for what Phase One should not attempt to do. Phase One should not attempt to address the operating dimensions. The temptation to address them is strong, because the operating dimensions are visible and the keystone is structural. The temptation should be resisted. Phase One is focused on the keystone. The operating dimensions wait for Phase Two.

WHY PHASE TWO COMES SECOND

Phase Two operationalizes the dimensions. The work cannot be undertaken before Phase One because the work requires the decision authority that Phase One establishes. Policies are operationally binding only when there is decision authority to enforce them. Controls are operationally effective only when there is decision authority to act on what the controls reveal. Risks are operationally managed only when there is decision authority to accept or escalate them. Vendor relationships are operationally governed only when there is decision authority to bind the vendor and to terminate when warranted. AI capabilities are operationally governed only when there is decision authority across the lifecycle. Incidents produce operational learning only when there is decision authority to act on the learning.

The Phase Two work is, in operational terms, the bulk of the visible governance modernization. The dimension chapters in Part Two describe what mature operation looks like in each dimension. Phase Two is the work to get each dimension from its current state to its Stage 3 or Stage 4 condition. The work is dimension-specific. The work is, in most cases, substantial. The work is also, in most cases, tractable once the Phase One foundation is in place.

WHY PHASE THREE COMES LAST

Phase Three constructs the learning systems. The systems require the operational maturity that Phase Two produces. A learning system requires evidence to learn from. The evidence is produced by the dimensions in operation. Before the dimensions are operating, the evidence is not available. The construction of learning systems before the dimensions are operating produces analytical infrastructure that has nothing to analyze.

Phase Three is, in operational terms, the work that distinguishes the Pacesetters from the cohort. The Pacesetters have, in most cases, completed substantial Phase Three work. The non-Pacesetters have, in most cases, not begun it. The differential between the two cohorts is, in most observations, the differential in learning systems rather than in any specific operating dimension.

WHAT HAPPENS IF THE SEQUENCE IS INVERTED

Organizations sometimes invert the sequence. The inversion is rarely deliberate. It typically emerges from local pressures that produce phase work out of sequence. A regulatory event forces Phase Two work on a specific dimension. A board concern requires Phase Three reporting capability. The work is undertaken because it must be undertaken, regardless of whether the sequencing logic supports it.

The consequences of the inversion are typically predictable. The out--of-sequence work produces partial improvement. The improvement is, in most cases, smaller than the resource investment would predict. The improvement is also typically not durable. The improvement, lacking the supporting work that the sequencing logic would have provided, erodes over the eighteen to twenty-four months following the work's completion. The investment has been made. The improvement has been realized. The improvement has not persisted. The cycle repeats with the next regulatory event or board concern.

> *Out-of-sequence work produces partial improvement that is, in most cases, not durable. The investment has been made. The persistence has not been established.*

The Pacesetters, in my observations, have generally followed the sequencing logic. Some have done so deliberately, having received assessment guidance similar to what this framework provides. Some have done so intuitively, having recognized that the structural work had to precede the operational work. The Pacesetter cohort is not characterized by an exceptional capacity for governance work. It is characterized by the sequencing of the work.

HOW THE PHASES INTERACT

The phases interact in ways that the simple sequential presentation does not capture. Phase One work in Decision Rights produces, as a byproduct, findings about the other dimensions. The findings inform Phase Two priorities. Phase Two work in any dimension produces, as a byproduct, evidence that should inform the other dimensions. The evidence flows into Phase Three. Phase Three work, conducted in any dimension, produces structural learning that feeds back into the other phases.

The interactions are productive when the sequencing is followed. The interactions are confusing when the sequencing is violated. Out-of-sequence Phase Three work has no Phase Two evidence to inform it; out-of-sequence Phase Two work has no Phase One foundation to support it. The interactions, in the inverted sequence, are not productive in the way the sequence assumes they should be.

◆ ◆ ◆

The next three chapters describe each phase in detail. The chapters are organized in the same way as the dimension chapters: what the phase is, what it produces, what the most common findings are, and what the executives undertaking the work can expect. The total volume of work is substantial. The volume is tractable. The work is, in 2026, the work that distinguishes the Pacesetters from the cohort. The chapters that follow describe how to do it.

CHAPTER IN BRIEF

- The remediation work is organized in three phases. Phase One (six months) addresses the keystone. Phase Two (twelve months) operationalizes the governance functions across operating dimensions. Phase Three (eighteen months) constructs the learning systems.
- Phase One must come first. The operating dimensions can be operationally strong only when the underlying decision rights are operationally strong. Strengthening the operating dimensions without first strengthening the keystone produces artifacts the organization can show without producing the governance the organization needs.
- Phase Three constructs the learning systems that distinguish the Pacesetters from the cohort. The systems require evidence from operating dimensions, which requires Phase Two completion.
- Inverted sequences produce partial, non-durable improvements that erode within eighteen to twenty-four months. The Pacesetter cohort is not characterized by exceptional governance capacity; it is characterized by sequencing.

CHAPTER XVI

Phase One: Fix the Keystone

"Six months is enough time to repair the foundation if you actually work on the foundation."
— from the methodology

Phase One is the work on Decision Rights. The phase runs six months. The phase produces, when executed well, an authority matrix that is current, extended for AI-specific decisions, operationally aligned with actual decision flow, exercised by the named authorities, and connected to the accountability flow when decisions produce consequences. The phase is the precondition for everything that follows.

This chapter describes the Phase One work in operational terms. What activities occur in each month. What decisions are required of the executive sponsor. What artifacts are produced. What resistance is typical and how to address it. The work is, in my experience, more political than technical. The political work is what makes the phase challenging. The methodology is well-defined.

THE PHASE ONE CHARTER

The phase begins with an executive charter. The charter establishes the work, names the executive sponsor, establishes the authority of the working team, and articulates the scope. The charter is not, in most cases, a one-page document. It is a substantive instrument that anticipates the political work the phase requires.

The charter typically includes: the executive sponsor (in most cases, the CEO, with the General Counsel and the chief audit executive as co-sponsors), the working team's authority (typically, the authority to interview any executive or program team, to access any documented authority artifact, and to recommend changes to the authority matrix subject to executive sponsor approval), the scope (extension and operational alignment of the authority matrix, with attention to AI-specific decision categories), the deliverables (revised matrix, operational alignment verification report, exception handling protocol, accountability flow documentation), and the timeline (six months from charter execution to deliverable acceptance).

The charter is the executive sponsor's commitment. The commitment is, in operational terms, what makes the work possible. Without the commitment, the working team will encounter resistance that they cannot, on their own, overcome. The commitment is exercised when the resistance arises. The exercise of the commitment by the executive sponsor is the signal to the organization that the work is to be taken seriously.

MONTHS ONE AND TWO: DISCOVERY

The first two months are discovery. The work includes: review of the current authority matrix, interviews with the named authorities about authority they believe they have, interviews with the program teams about authority they believe they exercise, comparison of the two sets of accounts, identification of the gaps, and prioritization of the gaps for remediation.

The discovery work is, in operational terms, substantial. The interviews require careful preparation. The interview discipline includes specific questions about authority categories, decision examples from the past twelve months, and the operational reality of how decisions have actually been made. The interview discipline is calibrated to produce candor without provoking defensive responses.

The discovery output is, in most cases, more substantial than the executive sponsor expected. The current authority matrix is found to be partial. The operational decision flow is found to diverge from the matrix in substantial ways. The AI-specific decision categories are found to be governed informally, in most cases, by whichever team is closest to the decision when it needs to be made. The discovery is not pleasant for the executive sponsor. The discovery is also the precondition for the work that follows.

MONTHS THREE AND FOUR: DESIGN

The next two months are design. The work includes: extension of the authority matrix to cover the discovered gaps (particularly the AI-specific decision categories), specification of the operational alignment between the matrix and the decision flow, design of the exception handling protocol, and design of the accountability flow documentation.

The design work is technical. The work requires substantive consideration of which decisions should be made at which authority levels, what approval pathways are appropriate, what exception thresholds make sense, and how the operational decision flow should be modified to match the matrix's specifications. The design is, in practice, substantially completed in the four months from discovery to design. The remaining work is implementation, which begins in month five.

The design produces a revised authority matrix. The matrix is, in practice, significantly different from the matrix the organization had at the beginning of the phase. The differences include: new decision categories addressing AI-specific decisions, revised authority levels for some existing decision categories where the discovered gap revealed misalignment, revised exception handling protocols where the discovered patterns revealed inadequacies, and revised accountability documentation that aligns with the matrix.

MONTHS FIVE AND SIX: IMPLEMENTATION

The final two months are implementation. The work includes: communication of the revised matrix to the bound populations, training of the named authorities on their authority and how to exercise it, modification of the operational decision workflows to match the matrix, and exercise of the new authority on actual decisions during the implementation period.

The implementation work is substantially political rather than technical. The communication has to be calibrated to produce both understanding and commitment. The training has to be substantive rather than perfunctory. The workflow modifications have to be operationally tested rather than just documented. The exercise of the new authority has to be supported, in early instances, by the executive sponsor's visible attention.

The implementation, by month six, has not, in practice, fully stabilized. The matrix is in place. The operational flow has been modified. The authorities are being exercised. The full stabilization requires another six to twelve months of operation. The continued attention to the implementation, after month six, is what makes the modifications durable.

THE MOST COMMON RESISTANCE

Phase One produces resistance. The resistance is, in operational reality, the resistance to the loss of informal authority that the matrix correction surfaces.

The resistance comes from teams that had been exercising authority that the matrix did not document. The teams had developed efficient operational patterns based on the informal authority. The new matrix, accurately specifying the documented authority, takes the informal authority back. The teams experience the change as a loss of operational efficiency. The teams resist.

The resistance is addressed by the executive sponsor's commitment. The sponsor, when the resistance surfaces, exercises the commitment by making clear that the matrix's specifications are to be followed regardless of the operational efficiency cost. The cost is, in most cases, substantially smaller than the team's resistance suggests. The cost is borne. The matrix's authority is established. The operational patterns adapt over time.

A second source of resistance comes from named authorities who, on receiving authority they had previously allowed to be exercised at lower levels, are reluctant to exercise it. The authorities had developed comfortable operational patterns in which they did not have to make decisions. The new matrix requires them to make decisions. The decisions are, in some cases, unfamiliar. The authorities resist.

This second resistance is addressed by training and by visible support from the executive sponsor. The training is substantive. The support is visible. The authorities, with training and support, learn to exercise the authority. The learning takes time. The time is built into the phase.

A third source of resistance comes from cultural patterns that have developed around the informal decision flow. The patterns may include rapid decision-making that the new matrix slows down, distributed decision-making that the new matrix concentrates, or speculative decision-making that the new matrix constrains. The patterns are valued by the people who operate within them. The new matrix is experienced as bureaucratic interference.

This third resistance is addressed by careful design of the matrix. The matrix is, when well-designed, not bureaucratic. The matrix is operationally efficient at the speed the operations require. The matrix is also operationally accurate, with authority residing where it actually should reside. The combination of efficiency and accuracy produces operational improvement rather than bureaucratic interference. The design work in months three and four is what makes this combination possible.

WHAT PHASE ONE PRODUCES

Phase One, executed well, produces several specific outcomes.

First, an authority matrix that is current and extended for AI-specific decisions. The matrix specifies, for the new decision categories, which authority is required, what approval pathway is appropriate, what exception thresholds apply, and what documentation is produced. The categories are no longer governed informally. They are governed under the matrix's specifications.

Second, operational alignment between the documented matrix and the actual decision flow. The gaps that the discovery surfaced are addressed. The matrix's specifications are operationally followed. The named authorities exercise the authority. The teams operating under the matrix make decisions within their scope. The matrix is, in operational reality, what it documents.

Third, accountability flow that aligns with the decision-making. When decisions produce consequences, the accountability flows to the parties who made the decisions. The flow requires the documentation that the decisions were made, by whom, and within what authority. The documentation is produced through the workflows that the matrix governs. The accountability is, when consequences materialize, traceable to the decision-makers.

Fourth, the foundation for Phase Two. The operating dimensions, in Phase Two, will be operationally strengthened. The strengthening requires the decision authority that Phase One establishes. The decision authority is, by the end of Phase One, in place.

◆ ◆ ◆

Phase One is the most consequential phase of the three. The phase is also the phase that, in my experience, organizations are most reluctant to undertake at the level of intensity the phase requires. The reluctance is understandable. The work is uncomfortable. The work is also the work without which the rest of the program cannot succeed. The reluctance is what the executive sponsor's commitment is required to overcome.

CHAPTER IN BRIEF

- Phase One runs six months and focuses on Decision Rights. The work is more political than technical; the methodology is well-defined, but the resistance is substantial.
- The phase begins with an executive charter that names the sponsor (typically CEO with General Counsel and chief audit executive as co-sponsors), establishes the working team's authority, and articulates scope and deliverables.
- The four-month arc of discovery and design produces a revised authority matrix substantially different from the one the organization began with. The final two months are implementation, with full stabilization continuing six to twelve months after the phase formally concludes.
- Resistance comes from three sources: teams losing informal authority, named authorities reluctant to exercise authority they had allowed to drift downward, and cultural patterns built around the prior informal flow. Each is addressable; none is incidental.

CHAPTER XVII

Phase Two: Operationalize Governance

"The visible work is the work the organization will eventually be measured on. It is not, however, the most important work."
— from the methodology

Phase Two is the visible phase. The work spans multiple dimensions and produces, over twelve months, the operational improvements that the dimension chapters in Part Two describe. The work is substantial. The work is also, in most cases, what the executive sponsor's stakeholders expect when they ask about the governance program. The dimension-by-dimension improvements are what they can recognize as governance work.

This chapter describes the Phase Two work across the six operating dimensions. The work is not undertaken simultaneously across all six. The dimensions are prioritized based on the Phase One findings and the assessment's diagnostic patterns. The chapter explains the prioritization logic, the typical work in each dimension, and what executives should expect from the phase.

PRIORITIZATION LOGIC

The Phase Two work is not undertaken simultaneously across all six operating dimensions. The simultaneity would exceed the organizational capacity to absorb change. The dimensions are prioritized based on three considerations: the Phase One findings (which dimensions have the most consequential gaps), the diagnostic patterns (which dimensions are most affected by the Locked-In and Unmodeled patterns), and the regulatory and competitive context (which dimensions face the most acute external pressure).

The typical prioritization in the advisory work this framework is designed to support places the dimensions in approximately the following order: AI Use and Lifecycle, Third-Party and Embedded AI, Controls, Risk, Policy, Incident. The order is not invariant. Specific organizations will produce different orderings based on their specific assessment findings. The order presented here is the modal case rather than the prescriptive case.

AI Use and Lifecycle comes first because the dimension is, at most enterprises, the most acutely weak. The dimension has been constructed most recently, has the largest scope gap relative to its actual footprint, and is the dimension most directly stressed by the technology the firm is deploying. The Phase Two work in this dimension produces the inventory completeness, the approval discipline, the monitoring infrastructure, and the lifecycle management that the dimension's mature state requires.

Third-Party and Embedded AI comes second because the dimension's AI-specific extensions are, at most enterprises, the most consequentially missing. The conventional vendor risk discipline exists. The AI extensions do not. The Phase Two work introduces the extensions: vendor-specific AI inventory, contractual provisions, vendor AI governance assessment, concentration analysis.

Controls comes third because the dimension's effectiveness measurement is, in most cases, the most analytically tractable improvement. The catalog review work, the effectiveness measurement work, the continuous monitoring construction work are well-defined methodologies. The work produces visible improvements in operational governance. The work also surfaces the Catalog-Inflation pattern that the dimension typically exhibits.

Risk, Policy, and Incident follow in approximately that order, with the specific ordering determined by the engagement's specific findings. Risk is prioritized when the register-without-decision pattern is severe. Policy is prioritized when the coverage-without-binding pattern is severe. Incident is prioritized when the learning-without-implementation pattern is severe.

WORK IN EACH DIMENSION

The Phase Two work in each dimension is dimension-specific. I will describe the work in summary form for each dimension, with the understanding that the specific work depends on the assessment findings for the specific organization.

AI USE AND LIFECYCLE

The work includes: comprehensive AI inventory discovery (extending beyond team submissions to include automated discovery and mandatory disclosure requirements), AI inventory classification (by risk tier and use case category), approval workflow design (including the explicit specification of behavior boundaries, training data conditions, use case scope, and monitoring requirements), monitoring infrastructure construction (including the response capability that converts monitoring outputs into action), lifecycle management documentation (including model update governance, fine-tuning governance, and decommissioning processes), and integration with the Phase One authority matrix.

THIRD-PARTY AND EMBEDDED AI

The work includes: comprehensive vendor inventory (including the fourth-party and beyond relationships), vendor classification with AI-specific attention, AI-specific contractual provisions for critical vendors (introduced through renegotiation), vendor AI governance assessment for critical vendors, concentration analysis with substitution planning, and integration with the Phase One authority matrix on vendor decisions.

CONTROLS

The work includes: catalog review against effectiveness criteria (retiring controls without evidence, redesigning controls with weak evidence), effectiveness measurement infrastructure construction (for the controls that remain), continuous monitoring discipline construction (with response playbooks, escalation pathways, and staffing model), and integration with the Phase One authority matrix on control exceptions.

RISK IDENTIFICATION

The work includes: methodology calibration against materialized risks (reviewing historical risks against the scoring methodology and adjusting for systematic bias), aggregation technique construction (stress testing, scenario analysis, concentration analysis, correlation analysis), decision integration (making the register operationally relevant at the points of decision), and integration with the Phase One authority matrix on risk acceptance.

POLICY

The work includes: policy library review against operational binding (retiring policies that produce no observable behavioral effect, revising policies with weak binding mechanisms), enforcement mechanism construction (monitoring of adherence, detection of deviation, escalation of material deviation, consequence application), exception management discipline construction (returning exception management to specified authority levels), and integration with the Phase One authority matrix on policy approval and exception authority.

INCIDENT MANAGEMENT

The work includes: detection capability extension into under-detected domains, investigation discipline deepening to include systemic examination, learning implementation tracking (with verification that recommendations have been implemented and have produced intended effect), and integration with the Phase One authority matrix on incident response authority.

WHAT PHASE TWO PRODUCES

Phase Two, executed well, produces dimension-specific operational improvements across the six operating dimensions. The improvements are visible. The improvements are measurable. The improvements are what the executive sponsor's stakeholders will recognize as governance modernization.

The improvements include, summarized across dimensions: a complete AI inventory with operating governance; vendor risk that addresses AI-specific concerns; a controls catalog that has been reviewed for effectiveness with infrastructure for ongoing effectiveness measurement; risk identification that informs consequential decisions with calibrated methodology; policy library that binds behavior with operational enforcement mechanisms; incident management that produces structural learning with verified implementation.

Each improvement is, individually, substantial. The combined effect is what the framework's Stage 4 condition looks like in operation. The combined effect is what the Pacesetters have, in most cases, achieved. The combined effect is what the non-Pacesetter cohort has not, in most cases, achieved.

COMMON PITFALLS

Phase Two has, in my experience, several common pitfalls.

The first is the temptation to undertake all six dimensions simultaneously. The temptation is understandable. All six dimensions have findings that warrant remediation. The simultaneity, however, exceeds the organizational capacity to absorb change. The work is, when undertaken simultaneously, undertaken partially in each dimension. The partial work in each dimension produces partial improvement that, lacking the supporting work, is not durable. The sequenced work, dimension by dimension, produces more durable improvement than the simultaneous work.

The second pitfall is the substitution of artifact production for operational change. The work in each dimension can be executed as artifact production (producing the documentation that demonstrates the work has occurred) or as operational change (producing the actual operational modifications the work is intended to produce). The two are not the same. The artifact production is easier and produces visible deliverables. The operational change is harder and produces less-visible operational reality. The phase, executed well, requires the operational change rather than the artifact production. The phase, executed poorly, produces artifact without the operational change.

The third pitfall is the failure to integrate with Phase One. The Phase Two work in each dimension depends on the Phase One authority matrix. The dependence is operational rather than nominal. The dimension-specific work has to be designed against the matrix's specifications. The work, when not designed against the matrix, produces dimension-specific improvements that operate in parallel to the matrix rather than in coordination with it. The parallel operation is not what the framework's Stage 4 condition requires.

WHAT COMES NEXT

Phase Two produces operational improvements across the operating dimensions. The improvements are substantial. They are also, by themselves, not sufficient for the framework's Stage 5 condition. Stage 5 requires the learning systems that Phase Three constructs. Without the learning systems, the Phase Two improvements are operationally strong and structurally static. The improvements, lacking the learning systems, will not, over time, improve themselves. The improvements will, over time, gradually erode as the organization's circumstances change and the improvements do not adapt.

◆ ◆ ◆

Phase Three constructs the learning systems. The phase is the work that distinguishes the Pacesetters from the cohort that has done substantial Phase Two work but has not constructed the systems that make the work durable. The next chapter describes the Phase Three work.

CHAPTER IN BRIEF

- Phase Two is the visible phase. Over twelve months, dimension-by-dimension operational improvements are produced across the six operating dimensions. The work is what stakeholders will recognize as governance modernization.
- The dimensions are prioritized based on Phase One findings, diagnostic patterns, and external pressure. The modal order is AI Use, Third-Party, Controls, Risk, Policy, Incident.
- The three common pitfalls are: simultaneous attempts on all dimensions (exceeding organizational absorption capacity), substitution of artifact production for operational change, and failure to integrate with the Phase One authority matrix.
- Phase Two produces Stage 4 operation. It does not, by itself, produce Stage 5 operation. The improvements are operationally strong and structurally static. Without the learning systems Phase Three constructs, they erode over time.

CHAPTER XVIII

Phase Three: Build Learning Systems

"The systems that survive are the systems that learn faster than their environment changes."
— Stafford Beer

Phase Three is the work most organizations do not do. The work is structural rather than operational. The work produces the systems that make the governance dimensions, in operation, capable of improving themselves. The work spans eighteen months. The work, when executed well, produces the framework's Stage 5 condition in the dimensions where the work is concentrated. The work is, in 2026, the work that distinguishes the Pacesetters from the cohort that has completed Phase Two but has not begun Phase Three.

This chapter describes the Phase Three work. The work is more abstract than the Phase Two work. The deliverables are less visible. The benefits accrue over a longer time horizon. The work is, in many ways, the most important work the framework recommends. It is also the work most likely to be deferred, because it does not, in the short term, produce the visible improvements that stakeholders can recognize.

THREE COMPONENTS

Phase Three has three components. The first is the construction of analytical capability that the Unmodeled pattern requires for remediation. The second is the construction of cross-dimensional integration that allows evidence from one dimension to drive structural change in another. The third is the construction of executive-level alignment work that the Misaligned pattern requires for remediation.

Each component runs for substantially the entire eighteen months. The components overlap. The components reinforce each other. The execution of all three, in coordination, produces the learning system that the framework's Stage 5 condition requires.

ANALYTICAL CAPABILITY

The first component is the construction of analytical capability. The capability is the ability to model the contribution of each governance function with operational specificity. The capability addresses the Unmodeled pattern by producing the analytical articulation that the pattern's signature element question requires.

The construction includes: the definition of contribution metrics for each governance function (what specifically does the function contribute, measured how), the construction of measurement infrastructure (collecting the data required to compute the metrics), the calibration of the metrics against benchmark performance (what does good look like for this metric), and the integration of the metrics into ongoing governance reporting (so the metrics inform decisions rather than just measure outcomes).

The work is substantial. The work is, at many firms, the construction of analytical capability that has never previously existed in the governance functions. The capability is, in some firms, available in adjacent functions (financial analysis, operational analysis, data science). The Phase Three work, when adjacent capability is available, may include the assignment of the adjacent capability to the governance functions or the construction of new capability dedicated to governance.

The capability, once constructed, transforms the governance functions. The functions can articulate their contribution. The functions can identify which components contribute more and which contribute less. The functions can prioritize their investment based on analytical evidence rather than political dynamics. The transformation is structural rather than operational. The functions, with the analytical capability, are different kinds of functions than the functions without it.

CROSS-DIMENSIONAL INTEGRATION

The second component is the construction of cross-dimensional integration. The integration allows evidence from one dimension to drive structural change in another. The integration is the operational mechanism that the framework's Stage 4 condition requires.

The construction includes: the definition of evidence flows between dimensions (what evidence from one dimension should inform what activities in another), the construction of operational mechanisms that route the evidence (workflows, dashboards, alerts), the establishment of accountability for the evidence flow (who is responsible for what evidence reaching what dimension), and the integration of the cross-dimensional evidence into the dimension-specific governance decisions.

The specific flows include: incident patterns informing control redesign, control failures informing risk register updates, risk materializations informing vendor risk methodology, vendor failures informing policy updates, policy bypasses informing decision rights review, and decision authority changes informing AI lifecycle approvals. Each flow is operationally substantial. The construction of each flow is, at many firms, a multi-month effort.

The integration, once constructed, produces the operating-as-a-system condition that the framework's Stage 4 requires. The dimensions, with the integration, are not independent functions. They are components of a coordinated governance system. The system operates with the cross-dimensional flows producing the coherent governance that the framework articulates as the mature state.

EXECUTIVE ALIGNMENT

The third component is the construction of executive-level alignment. The work addresses the Misaligned pattern by producing the explicit alignment that the pattern's signature element question requires.

The construction includes: facilitated alignment sessions among the named executives (with the assessment findings as the substantive basis for the sessions), the articulation of explicit alignment statements (what governance is for, what risks it should mitigate, what success looks like), the integration of the alignment statements into ongoing executive committee discourse (so the alignment is operative rather than nominal), and the periodic revisitation of the alignment as circumstances change (so the alignment adapts to the organization's evolving condition).

The work is, in operational terms, executive coaching combined with structured facilitation. The work requires the executive sponsor's continuing engagement. The work requires the named executives' willingness to surface and address their misalignments. The work is, in practice, the most politically delicate work of the entire program. The work is also, in practice, the work that produces the most durable improvements in the governance program's effectiveness.

The alignment, once constructed, is not permanent. Executive teams change. Circumstances evolve. The alignment requires ongoing maintenance. The maintenance work, after the initial Phase Three construction, becomes part of the executive committee's standing operation. The maintenance is, when done well, brief but regular. The brief regular maintenance prevents the gradual re-emergence of the Misaligned condition.

WHAT PHASE THREE PRODUCES

Phase Three, executed well, produces the framework's Stage 5 condition in the dimensions where the work is concentrated. The dimensions, in this condition, are operating, integrated with adjacent dimensions, and improving over time based on evidence from their own operation. The dimensions learn. The dimensions adapt. The dimensions become, over time, more effective at the governance work they were constructed to do.

The Stage 5 condition is, in 2026, what the Pacesetter cohort has substantially achieved in several dimensions. The Stage 5 condition is, in 2026, what the non-Pacesetter cohort has not, in most cases, begun to achieve. The differential between the two cohorts is, in substantial part, the differential between the Stage 5 condition and the lower stages.

The Pacesetter advantage, observable in the differential AI returns, is the operational consequence of the Stage 5 condition. The condition produces governance that is, in operation, generating evidence about its own effectiveness and updating itself in response. The condition produces, over time, governance that is better at producing the outcomes governance is supposed to produce. The condition produces, over five years, governance that has matured into substantially superior performance compared to governance that has not, in the same period, undertaken the Phase Three work.

THE THREE-YEAR HORIZON

The three phases together span thirty-six months. The thirty-six months are not, in operational terms, the end of the work. The work continues, after the phases conclude, as the ongoing operation of the mature governance system. The work after the phases is qualitatively different. The work before the phases is construction. The work during the phases is construction and operational improvement. The work after the phases is operational improvement and adaptive maintenance.

The thirty-six months are, in my experience, the time it takes for an enterprise that begins the work at a typical starting state to reach the Pacesetter condition. The condition, once reached, is sustainable with substantially less effort than the construction required. The maintenance is approximately twenty to thirty percent of the construction effort. The benefits, once the construction is complete, accrue with the maintenance investment rather than the construction investment.

The window for the construction, as I argued in Chapter 3, is open in 2026 and will not remain open indefinitely. Enterprises that begin the construction in 2026 can complete it by 2029. Enterprises that begin in 2027 will complete it by 2030. Enterprises that have not begun by 2028 will, in my judgment, find the Pacesetter cohort's lead difficult to close.

◆ ◆ ◆

The next part of the book is the conclusion. The conclusion describes the choice the executive readers face. The choice is, in the analytical sense, simple. The doing is harder. The doing is what this book has been about.

CHAPTER IN BRIEF

- Phase Three runs eighteen months and constructs three things: analytical capability that addresses the Unmodeled pattern, cross-dimensional integration that allows evidence from one dimension to drive structural change in another, and executive-level alignment that addresses the Misaligned pattern.
- The work is more abstract than Phase Two. The deliverables are less visible. The benefits accrue over a longer time horizon. The work is also the work most likely to be deferred.
- Phase Three produces the framework's Stage 5 condition. Stage 5 in 2026 is what the Pacesetter cohort has substantially achieved in several dimensions. It is what the non-Pacesetter cohort has not, in most cases, begun to achieve.
- The three phases together span thirty-six months. Enterprises that begin the construction in 2026 can complete it by 2029. The window for construction will not remain open indefinitely.

CONCLUSION

The Choice Between Two Futures

"The future is already here. It's just not very evenly distributed."
— William Gibson

This book has been an argument. The argument has been that enterprise governance, designed for a different era of technology, has been quietly outflanked by the technology that has entered the enterprise over the past decade. The outflanking has produced a structural gap between the governance enterprises document and the governance they actually operate. The gap is widening. The gap is also, for organizations willing to undertake the work, addressable.

The argument has had three layers. The diagnostic layer described the gap and how it emerged. The framework layer described the analytical instrument for measuring an organization's specific condition relative to the gap. The remediation layer described the work to close the gap.

The argument leaves the reader at a choice. The choice is between two futures. The book ends with the choice articulated as plainly as I can articulate it.

THE FIRST FUTURE

The first future is the future in which the enterprise does not undertake the work this book describes. The enterprise continues to invest in AI. The enterprise continues to produce governance documentation. The enterprise continues to satisfy the audiences that evaluate governance from the outside. The enterprise also, over time, accumulates the cumulative consequences of the gap between the documentation and the operation. The consequences include partial returns on the AI investment, recurring incidents that do not produce structural learning, regulatory exposures that widen over time, vendor concentrations that become operationally consequential when stressed, and a gradual erosion of competitive position relative to the Pacesetter cohort.

This future is not catastrophic. The enterprise continues to operate. The operation is, in most quarters, satisfactory. The deterioration is slow. The deterioration is, viewed quarter by quarter, plausibly attributable to other factors. The deterioration is, viewed over five years, substantially attributable to the cumulative consequence of the governance work the enterprise did not undertake.

This future is what most enterprises will have. The cohort behind the Pacesetters will continue to be behind. Some will fall further behind. A few will fail. Most will continue, producing partial returns, satisfying their stakeholders to a degree, and gradually losing ground to competitors that did the work.

THE SECOND FUTURE

The second future is the future in which the enterprise undertakes the work. The work begins with an honest assessment. The assessment produces uncomfortable findings. The findings are received by an executive team prepared to act on them. The Phase One work addresses the keystone. The Phase Two work operationalizes the dimensions. The Phase Three work constructs the learning systems. The work spans thirty-six months.

At the end of the thirty-six months, the enterprise is in the Pacesetter cohort. The cohort's advantages accrue. The AI investment produces material returns. The governance, in operation, is generating evidence about its own effectiveness and updating itself in response. The enterprise's competitive position relative to the cohort that did not do the work is, by the end of the thirty-six months, substantially better than it was at the beginning. The position continues to improve in subsequent years.

This future is not utopian. The work is hard. The work produces, along the way, surfacing of dysfunction that the enterprise had been comfortable to leave unsurfaced. The work produces political resistance that the executive sponsor has to address. The work produces, in some cases, executive departures and other disruptions that the enterprise has to absorb. The work is consequential because the conditions it addresses are consequential.

This future is what the Pacesetters have. They are not, in most cases, organizations of exceptional capacity. They are organizations that have done the work. The doing of the work is what distinguishes them. The work is available to other organizations that are willing to undertake it.

THE CHOICE

The choice between the two futures is, in the analytical sense, easy. The second future is, by every operational measure, better than the first. The benefits of the second exceed the costs of the work that produces it. The benefits accrue with compounding advantage. The doing is, however, harder. The work is uncomfortable. The political dynamics are real. The investment in time and attention is substantial. Many organizations will, on full consideration, decide that the work is more disruption than the organization can absorb.

I have written this book in the hope that some organizations will decide otherwise. The Pacesetter cohort is, in 2026, roughly one in five of the enterprises ServiceNow surveyed. The cohort can grow. The conditions that produce membership in the cohort are not exclusive. The work is available to any organization willing to undertake it. The choice is the executive team's.

If you are the executive making the choice, I will end with three observations.

First, the work is more tractable than it appears from outside. The methodology is well-defined. The patterns are recognizable. The phases are well-bounded. The work is not, in operational reality, mysterious. The work is hard because it is uncomfortable, not because it is technically difficult.

Second, the work produces compounding returns. The early returns are visible by month twelve. The middle returns accrue across years two and three. The structural returns continue to compound for years after the formal program completes. The returns are not, in most cases, fully appreciated until they have been compounding for several years. The decision to begin is the decision that, more than any other, determines the returns.

Third, the work is more interesting than it appears from outside. The surfacing of the patterns is, for executives accustomed to abstract governance discussion, often startling. The conversations the work produces are, in my experience, among the most substantive conversations executive teams have. The work is, when undertaken, intellectually rewarding in addition to being operationally consequential.

◆ ◆ ◆

The two futures are not, in any deterministic sense, fated. The choice between them is real. The work to produce the second is available. The window is open.

The work is more tractable than it appears from outside. The methodology is well-defined. The patterns are recognizable. The work is hard because it is uncomfortable, not because it is technically difficult.

◆ ◆ ◆

APPENDIX A

Sample Diagnostic Questions

This appendix presents selected representative questions from each dimension of the framework. They illustrate the framework's diagnostic logic and the level of operational specificity the assessment seeks. They are not the assessment instrument.

What is not disclosed here is the rest of what makes the framework diagnostic. The interview discipline that produces candor under conditions of confidentiality. The cross-source triangulation among program teams, executives, and documentary evidence that prevents any single account from going unchecked. The dimension-by-dimension scoring methodology that translates responses into stage assignments. The floor and gap rules that prevent averaging from flattering its subjects. The pattern-detection logic that surfaces the four cumulative diagnostic patterns from the Section E findings. The remediation sequencing that converts the diagnosis into a phased plan of work. These are the components in which the framework's analytical value resides. They are applied through the engagement methodology and are not adequately conveyed by question text alone.

A practitioner who used only the questions reproduced here, without the rest of the methodology, would produce some useful conversation and would not produce a diagnosis. The questions are the surface. The framework is what sits below them.

POLICY AND ENFORCEMENT

When was a policy in the current library last revised specifically because evidence from the policy program's own operation indicated revision was warranted?

Does the program team privately believe that a current policy is ineffective and persists for organizational reasons? If so, what policy, and what dynamics prevent its change?

If the policy program were eliminated tomorrow, what specific behaviors would change? In which populations? With what likelihood and consequence?

(Asked separately of CEO, General Counsel, and Chief Compliance Officer) What is the policy program for, in your view? What are the three most important things it should produce?

How is exception management authority exercised in practice? Where the operational practice diverges from the documented authority, what accounts for the divergence?

RISK IDENTIFICATION AND ASSESSMENT

Has the risk identification methodology been revised in the past twelve months specifically because of evidence from the program's own operation? Please describe the specific revision and the evidence that drove it.

Is the risk team privately aware of a risk that has not been escalated for organizational reasons? Please describe (under conditions of confidentiality).

(Asked separately of CEO, CRO, CFO, and the board chair) What are the top five risks the organization faces? What are the criteria by which you ranked them?

For each of the three most consequential risks materialized in the past thirty-six months, what pre- materialization score did the risk register carry? What does the comparison reveal about the methodology's calibration?

Where the register and the consequential decision flow intersect, what is the operational mechanism by which the register's content actually informs the decisions?

CONTROLS, EVIDENCE, AND CONTINUOUS MONITORING

Has a control been retired in the past twelve months specifically for proven ineffectiveness? Please describe the control, the evidence of ineffectiveness, and the retirement process.

For the three most expensive controls in the catalog, what evidence demonstrates that each control is, in fact, reducing the risk it nominally addresses?

Has the program identified, through structured exercise, controls it privately believes are ineffective but that persist for organizational reasons? Please describe.

(Asked separately of chief audit executive, CISO, and CIO) What are the five most critical controls in the organization? What criteria did you apply?

Of the monitoring outputs produced in the past ninety days, what fraction produced operational action? What accounts for the fraction that did not?

THIRD-PARTY AND EMBEDDED AI RISK

Has a critical vendor been terminated in the past twenty-four months for governance reasons? If not, what is the operational meaning of the program's termination authority?

Is the vendor risk team privately aware of vendor concerns that have not been escalated for organizational reasons? Please describe.

(Asked separately of CIO, CRO, General Counsel, and Chief Procurement Officer) What are the five most critical vendor relationships in the firm? What criteria did you apply?

What is the discovery methodology by which the firm identifies AI capabilities embedded in software contracted for non-AI purposes? When was the methodology last applied comprehensively?

For each of the three most critical AI vendors, what is the documented substitution plan? When was it last reviewed against current operational reality?

AI USE AND LIFECYCLE GOVERNANCE

Has an AI capability been decommissioned in the past twelve months for evidence-based reasons (rather than because the underlying vendor relationship changed)? Please describe.

Is the AI governance team privately aware of deployed AI capabilities that should not, on current understanding, be running? Please describe.

(Asked separately of CEO, CIO, CRO, and Chief Data Officer) What is the AI governance program for, in your view? What should success look like in twenty-four months?

For each of the five highest-risk AI capabilities currently in production, what behavior boundaries, training data conditions, and monitoring requirements were specified at the time of approval? Are subsequent operations being evaluated against those specifications?

What is the operational difference between the AI inventory the firm maintains and the AI footprint the firm actually has? When was the difference last assessed?

INCIDENT AND ISSUE MANAGEMENT

Has a structural change in the past twelve months been driven specifically by incident evidence (rather than by audit finding or executive directive)? Please describe the incident, the change, and the causal connection.

Is the incident program team privately aware of incidents whose structural implications were not, in the end, addressed? Please describe (under conditions of confidentiality).

(Asked separately of the CISO, COO, General Counsel, and Head of HR) What does incident-related accountability mean in this organization?

Of the recommendations produced by incident investigations in the past twenty-four months, what fraction have been verified as implemented and producing intended effect?

For the three most consequential incidents in the past thirty-six months, what was the systemic examination beyond the proximate cause? What contributory factors in adjacent dimensions were identified?

DECISION RIGHTS AND ACCOUNTABILITY

Has the authority matrix been revised in the past twelve months because evidence from its operation indicated revision was warranted? Please describe.

Where the documented authority matrix and the operational decision flow diverge, what accounts for the divergence? What is the operational meaning of the documented authority?

(Asked separately of named authorities) Please describe a recent example of a decision you made under the matrix's specifications. Please describe a recent example of a decision where you exercised escalation or declination authority.

(Asked separately of program teams) Please describe a recent example of a decision your team made. Under what documented authority did the team make it?

For the AI-specific decision categories that have emerged since the matrix was last comprehensively revised, what authority is documented? Where the authority is not documented, who is, in operational practice, making the decisions?

A NOTE ON THE SECTION E QUESTIONS

Several of the questions above will be recognizable, in form, as dimension-specific instances of the signature element described in Chapter 12. The recognition is intended. Section E does the framework's most consequential diagnostic work, and these illustrative questions give the reader a sense of what its interrogation looks like in a particular dimension.

Their analytical power, however, does not reside in the question text. It resides in the conditions under which the questions are asked, the cross-interview comparison the executive alignment finding requires, and the pattern-recognition logic that the aggregated responses feed. Readers who attempt to apply these questions in a Sunday-afternoon exercise will find them suggestive. Readers who want diagnostic findings should engage them with the methodology that makes the findings reliable.

APPENDIX B

A Sample Maturity Profile

This appendix presents a sample maturity profile in the form a client receives at the conclusion of a typical assessment engagement. The profile is notional. It does not derive from any specific engagement. It illustrates the form of the output and the kind of finding the assessment produces. It is included so that readers considering a formal engagement can see what they would receive.

The profile that follows depicts a mid-sized enterprise (the kind of organization where the framework is most often applied) approximately three years into its AI program. The profile reflects what I would call a modal case in 2026: substantial investment, some genuine maturity in places, and the characteristic patterns of the non-Pacesetter cohort. The narrative findings are summarized; the underlying evidence and the full pattern analysis are not reproduced here.

Readers should not interpret the specific stage assignments as prescriptive. Different organizations score differently, and the framework's value comes from the diagnostic specificity of the findings rather than from the numerical scores in isolation.

Policy and Enforcement .... Stage 2 — Defined

Library is thorough and current. Enforcement mechanisms are weak; exception management has drifted below specified authority levels. Documentation Theater pattern present.

Risk Identification and Assessment .... Stage 2 — Defined

Register is maintained but operates parallel to consequential decisions. Scoring methodology has not been calibrated against materialized risks in the past five years.

Controls, Evidence, and Continuous Monitoring .... Stage 3 — Managed

Catalog operates on schedule. Effectiveness measurement is largely absent; three controls retired in twenty-four months, all for audit-driven reasons rather than ineffectiveness evidence. Catalog inflation pattern present.

Third-Party and Embedded AI Risk .... Stage 1 — Reactive

Conventional vendor risk operates at Stage 3; AI-specific extensions are absent. Embedded AI inventory shows footprint approximately three times the formal inventory.

AI Use and Lifecycle Governance .... Stage 2 — Defined

Governance committee operates quarterly. Inventory is incomplete in the embedded-AI category. Approval criteria do not specify behavior boundaries; monitoring infrastructure exists in three of seventeen high-risk capabilities.

Incident and Issue Management .... Stage 2 — Defined

Cybersecurity incidents are well-detected; non-technical incidents are under-detected. Investigations consistently stop at proximate cause. Recommendations are documented but implementation is not verified.

Decision Rights and Accountability .... Stage 1 — Reactive

Authority matrix is current for financial decisions; absent or partial for AI-specific decision categories. Operational decision flow diverges substantially from documented authority in eleven of fourteen examined categories.

Figure 2. Sample maturity profile (notional). The full engagement output includes evidence references, pattern analysis, and a phased remediation roadmap.

CUMULATIVE PATTERN DIAGNOSIS

The dimension scores alone tell a partial story. The framework's analytical output includes the cumulative pattern diagnosis described in Chapter 13. For the notional profile above, the pattern diagnosis would read approximately as follows:

"The organization exhibits the Documentation Theater pattern in mature form across Policy, Risk, and Controls; the Locked-In pattern in early form across Risk and Controls; the Unmodeled pattern across all six operating dimensions; and the Misaligned pattern in nascent form across AI Use and Decision Rights. The cumulative diagnosis warrants a full three-phase remediation program, beginning with Phase One work on Decision Rights and continuing through Phase Two and Phase Three over the subsequent thirty months. The Decision Rights dimension is the binding constraint on improvement in the operating dimensions; without addressing it first, investments in the operating dimensions will produce documentation rather than governance."

The diagnosis is what makes the dimension scores actionable. Without it, the executive team sees that Decision Rights is at Stage 1 and AI Use is at Stage 2. With it, the executive team sees what those scores mean operationally, which patterns they produce in combination, and what the sequenced work to address them looks like. The diagnosis is the engagement's central deliverable. The dimension scores are the input.

WHAT THE FULL ENGAGEMENT OUTPUT INCLUDES

The complete output a client receives includes substantially more than the abbreviated profile reproduced here. The full deliverables include: the dimension-by-dimension maturity assessment with stage assignments and evidence references; the section-level findings within each dimension, including the floor and gap rule applications; the cumulative pattern diagnosis with the supporting evidence trail; the executive alignment analysis from the separate executive interviews; the prioritized roadmap for Phase One through Phase Three remediation; and the executive readout deck designed for board and executive committee presentation.

The engagement is also designed to surface findings the client did not anticipate. These emerge from the cross-source triangulation, where the program teams' accounts, the executives' separate accounts, and the documentary evidence are placed against each other in a structured way. The findings that result are, in practice, the most consequential output. They surface conditions that the executive team had not previously named, sometimes because the team had not previously been in a setting where naming them was possible. The naming is, in the engagement's structure, what makes the subsequent work possible.

APPENDIX C

Sources and Suggested Reading

This appendix has two purposes. The first is to document the empirical and analytical sources that establish the problem the framework addresses: the structural inadequacy of conventional governance for autonomous AI, the differential outcomes the ServiceNow research identified, the regulatory environment now hardening, and the related market signals. The second is to suggest reading for practitioners who want to deepen their understanding of the management and governance traditions on which the framework draws.

SOURCES FOR THE PROBLEM STATEMENT

ServiceNow. Enterprise AI Maturity Index 2025 (with Oxford Economics) and Enterprise AI Maturity Index 2026 (with ThoughtLab). Available at servicenow.com/standard/resource-center/white-paper/wp-enterprise-ai-maturity-index-2025.html and servicenow.com/content/dam/servicenow- assets/public/en-us/doc-type/resource-center/white-paper/wp-enterprise-ai-maturity-index- 2026.pdf. The empirical basis for the Pacesetter divergence on which Chapter 3 relies. The 2025 Index surveyed approximately 4,500 executives across sixteen countries and eleven industries, measuring AI maturity across five pillars (AI strategy and leadership, workflow integration, talent and workforce, AI governance, and AI investment) and identifying a Pacesetter cohort of 18.2% of respondents. The 2026 Index surveyed approximately 4,500 executives and, for the first time, 2,000 employees across nineteen countries and twelve industries, measuring maturity across seven pillars (vision and leadership; management and culture; data modernization; AI governance; talent and skills; AI-enabled workflows; and driving value from AI), identifying a Pacesetter cohort of 21% of respondents. ServiceNow defines the Pacesetter cohort not by budget or industry but by orchestration, connected data, and governance built before deployment rather than after. The framing of the Pacesetter divergence used in this book reflects the author's interpretation of the research and is supported by, but not identical to, ServiceNow's published language.

National Institute of Standards and Technology. Artificial Intelligence Risk Management Framework (AI RMF 1.0), NIST AI 100-1. January 26, 2023. Available at nvlpubs.nist.gov/nistpubs/ai/NIST.AI.100- 1.pdf (DOI: 10.6028/NIST.AI.100-1). The foundational US regulatory framework for AI risk management. Establishes the vocabulary that the framework's AI dimensions extend, particularly in characterizing the four properties (speed, opacity, scale, mutability) that distinguish AI from prior waves of enterprise technology.

International Organization for Standardization. ISO/IEC 42001:2023, Information technology — Artificial intelligence — Management system. Published December 18, 2023. Available at iso.org/standard/42001. The first international management system standard for AI. Provides the methodological structure that the framework's AI Use and Lifecycle dimension complements.

European Union. Regulation (EU) 2024/1689 of the European Parliament and of the Council laying down harmonised rules on artificial intelligence (AI Act). Official Journal of the European Union, July 12, 2024. Available at eur-lex.europa.eu/eli/reg/2024/1689/oj. The first comprehensive AI regulation. Informs the regulatory tightening that Chapter 3 identifies as one of the three forces closing the window.

United States Department of the Treasury. Managing Artificial Intelligence-Specific Cybersecurity Risks in the Financial Services Sector. March 27, 2024. Available at home.treasury.gov (Office of Cybersecurity and Critical Infrastructure Protection). Establishes the regulatory direction for AI risk management in US financial services and supports the discussion in Chapter 1 of the regulatory environment now arriving.

Federal Reserve and Office of the Comptroller of the Currency. Supervisory Guidance on Model Risk Management (SR 11-7 / OCC 2011-12), April 4, 2011. Available at federalreserve.gov/supervisionreg/srletters/sr1107.htm and occ.gov, with successor guidance from the FDIC and other regulators. The foundational US banking regulatory guidance on model risk. Provides historical context for the model-risk-management discipline that the AI dimensions extend.

MARKET AND INDUSTRY SIGNALS

Gartner. Enterprise AI Adoption and Maturity research streams, 2024–2026. The analyst research that has progressively quantified the gap between AI investment and realized returns. Useful for executives wanting market-level evidence beyond the ServiceNow research.

Forrester. The State of AI Governance, 2024–2026 research streams. Complementary analyst coverage that has tracked the maturation of AI governance practice across industries.

Cyber Insurance Market Reports, multiple carriers, 2024–2026. The cyber insurance market's tightening over the past five years is documented across the major carriers' annual reports and provides the empirical basis for the analogous tightening of AI liability insurance that Chapter 3 anticipates.

ON GOVERNANCE MATURITY

Humphrey, Watts S. "Characterizing the Software Process: A Maturity Framework." IEEE Software, vol. 5, no. 2, 1988, pp. 73–79. The foundational paper that established the maturity model tradition the framework's five-stage scale extends.

Software Engineering Institute, Carnegie Mellon University. CMMI for Services, Version 1.3. November 2010. The mature articulation of the CMMI tradition. Provides the structural inspiration for the five-stage scale and the floor-rule discipline.

Argyris, Chris. Organizational Traps: Leadership, Culture, Organizational Design. Oxford University Press, 2010. Argyris's analysis of how organizations fail to learn from evidence is foundational to the framework's signature element. His earlier work on single- and double-loop learning is similarly relevant.

ON RISK AND CONTROL

Kaplan, Robert S., and Anette Mikes. "Managing Risks: A New Framework." Harvard Business Review, June 2012. Articulates the categorical distinction between preventable, strategy, and external risks that informs the framework's risk dimension.

Taleb, Nassim Nicholas. Antifragile: Things That Gain from Disorder. Random House, 2012. The discussion of fragility and antifragility informs the framework's treatment of learning systems and the Phase Three work.

ON DECISION-MAKING AND ACCOUNTABILITY

Drucker, Peter F. The Effective Executive. Harper & Row, 1967. Drucker's articulation of the relationship between authority and responsibility remains foundational. The framework's keystone principle draws on Drucker's analysis.

Beer, Stafford. Brain of the Firm. Allen Lane, 1972. Beer's cybernetic analysis of viable systems informs the framework's treatment of learning systems and the framework's central premise that the purpose of a system is what it does.

Grove, Andrew S. Only the Paranoid Survive. Doubleday, 1996. Grove's articulation of strategic inflection points and the executive response to them informs the framework's argument about the present window for governance modernization.

Handy, Charles. The Age of Unreason. Harvard Business School Press, 1989. Handy's analysis of organizational change informs the book's argument about the difference between what organizations formally are and what they actually do.

Index of Key Concepts

About the Author

Justus Daniel Eapen spent the better part of two decades inside enterprise technology and governance across multiple industries, including service as a Chief Information Officer. He built the kinds of governance programs this book examines, sat through the audit committee briefings, chaired the AI governance committees that produced documentation rather than governance, and accumulated the operational frustrations that the framework was designed to resolve. His subsequent executive roles gave him the additional vantage point of evaluating governance artifacts from the position of the executives nominally responsible for them.

He is the founder of Orchestris Autonomous IT, a consulting practice that advises boards and executive teams on enterprise governance, decision rights, and the structural integration of artificial intelligence into operations. The Integrated Risk and AI Governance Maturity Model is the proprietary framework around which the practice is organized. The framework is designed for application across financial services, healthcare, technology, and other industries in which the autonomous enterprise is taking shape.

◆ ◆ ◆

He divides his time between the United States and India.

ORCHESTRIS AUTONOMOUS IT

orchestrisai.com

www.ingramcontent.com/pod-product-compliance
Lightning Source LLC
LaVergne TN
LVHW022215200926
848481LV00006B/1978